LIVING THE WORD

Tom Clancy

Living the Word

REFLECTIONS ON THE GOSPELS
OF THE THREE-YEAR CYCLE

the columba press

First published in 1996 by
the columba press
93 The Rise, Mount Merrion, Blackrock, Co Dublin

Cover by Bill Bolger
Origination by The Columba Press
Printed in Ireland by Colour Books Ltd, Dublin

ISBN 1 85607 156 1

Contents

YEAR B

YEAR C

Preface

The need for adult catechesis on an ever-widening variety of topics is putting increasing pressure on Sunday homily time. Too frequently, the Word is just read and left to one side, to make way for an exposition on a current issue of more or less importance. This is to be regretted. The Word proclaimed during the Eucharistic celebration has a unique role in fostering belief and inspiring conversions, even little ones. Reflection on this Word is the food of our faith. To whet the appetite for such nourishment, I write a weekly reflection in *The Cork Examiner*. From these reflections, I have selected one for each Sunday and some other occasions in the three-year cycle.

Many readers and friends have encouraged me to continue the ongoing newspaper contributions. I appreciate their continuing support.

My thanks to the management and editorial team of *The Cork Examiner* for facilitating the venture and for their competent and kind co-operation.

My thanks to Seán O Boyle and the staff of The Columba Press, whose personal commitment to religious publishing and unfailing courtesy to authors and customers ensure that it is a joy to work with them. I hope that you enjoy the result of our partnership and are somehow inspired by it for the daily living of the gospel.

Tom Clancy

Year A

First Sunday of Advent

Mt 24:37-44

Stay alert. Stay alive. The succinct warning to road users becomes more urgent daily as winter deepens and the festive season is rushed upon us. But the safety slogan can have a much wider significance for all Christians. Our calling is to be alert to the speed with which many much-sought-after goodies pass away like the morning fog. It may be popularity, possessions, power or pleasure. Even God's great gifts of health and life do not last forever. The only thing that lasts is relationship, our relationship with one another and in turn with God.

True success in life is living in right relationship. Sunday's gospel message is to be alert to anything and everything that undermines such living. Being so alert, we stay alive in God's love.

But the Christian message is not self-centred. Our calling is to alert the whole world to this mystery and we can do it only by how we live ourselves. Our times long for living witnesses to the gospel rather than for mere preachers or teachers. What example will we give this coming Christmas? Somebody will notice and somebody will be affected by our choice. Stay alert to the opportunities for generous love that come our way. It is the way to stay fully alive.

Second Sunday of Advent

Mt 3:1-12

Some young people resent it. Others thrive on it. Most trade on it when it suits. Introducing somebody as the off-spring of well-known or successful parents often ensures a ready acceptance in business and social circles. However useful this may be, the young sometimes want to retain their own unique identity and to live life from their own resources. The Jews of Jesus' time certainly did not belong to this latter category as today's gospel shows John the Baptist slating them for using their Father Abraham's reputation to guarantee salvation, no matter what their own lifestyle was like. True enough, Abraham was very special. He was chosen by God to be the Father of his very own people and he was blessed in a thousand ways. His descendants went overboard in crediting Abraham with such status that every one of his children was guaranteed salvation. They were wrong.

John the Baptist pointed out starkly that there is no such guarantee for anybody. God has no grand-children. We cannot cash in on the good works of those who went before us. Each generation, each individual, must accept the faith opportunity God offers them and make the most of it. As St Paul puts it today: 'It can only be to God's glory, then, for you to treat each other in the same friendly way as Christ treated you.'

Third Sunday of Advent

Mt 11:2-11

It happens in many a person's life. Certainty gives way to doubts, enthusiasm for a cause is replaced by a need for reassurance, commitment is undermined by a sense of being betrayed. It happened to John the Baptist. The fiery preacher who challenged the life style even of kings now wonders whether it was all in vain. The great forerunner of the Messiah wonders did he back the wrong man and give his life to a foolish cause. From his prison cell, he pleads with his cousin to intervene to renew his hope and restore his inner peace. Jesus moves to do just that. He sends the Baptist reports of his own life style with its care of the sick and the poor, its miracles of healing with its preaching of God's kingdom of forgiveness and new beginnings.

It was not what John expected from a Messiah but it was what God intended the Messiah to be. John understands, accepts and is renewed even to the heroic surrender of his life. In our time, many people have such Baptist moments and some people have them often over the years. The certainties of another time yield to the searching of a changing world. For some, the trusted ones seem to have betrayed the cause.

Who will confirm our faith and rekindle our hope? The answer is simple. From our prisons of fear, failure, sin, selfishness or doubt, we must send word to our Brother that we need him. That he will surely come to us with all his healing love and reassurance is as certain as the dawn. Prepare the way together.

Fourth Sunday of Advent

Mt 1:18-24

Mick was an old man when I first met him. He was known to most people as the Fox, though many never knew why. Some thought that he must have been redhaired in his youth. For others, it was just his name and the reason never bothered them, but for those who knew his life story the name was loaded with meaning. He has served as a soldier in the Far East. His company was trapped behind enemy lines. More than anything else, it was Mick's cunning and courage that enabled them to survive. He foraged for food. He explored escape routes. He was always alert to danger. To his companions, he was like a fox. The name kept his character and his feats alive for them.

When Joseph was told that his wife was to have a son whom she must call Jesus, he surely wondered why. Considering all the circumstances, would it not be better to call him Joseph and keep the family name alive? The name Jesus had overtones. It meant Saviour. Was the choice of name meant to tell something about what this child would be? Yes. The expected boy was to save the people from the evil of selfishness and to lead them to the fullness of love, human and divine. His name was to keep alive for us his saving role in our lives. The name of Jesus is truly a holy name, worthy of reverence and love. It is full of meaning for those who know the life story of the man.

As we hear in Sunday's gospel, the name was given to Joseph for the son of Mary, born for us at the first Christmas.

Christmas Day

Lk 2:1-14

For many coming home never loses its excitement. The prospect of welcome, warmth, and the renewal of love, can energise one's whole being. Some are never able to come. Some choose never to come even when there is someone waiting for them to come. Christmas is when most come. Some cannot come all the way themselves and somebody from home goes to meet them. Such a journey is never a burden but always a joy.

While most people belong to some family or neighbourly home, there are still many who are homeless this Christmas. Some of them have a place to live but the loneliness destroys the home-liness. Others, like the Lord Jesus, have not place to lay their heads and experience the rejection of there being no room in the inn for them. To create a society where every person is at home is a basic Christian duty at Christmas and always.

To be at home is to be where one feels one belongs, where the vulnerable one feels most secure, where the successful one is loved rather than acclaimed, where failure is forgiven, where trust evokes new beginnings, where the joy of being related is celebrated, where the bonds bind together to face adversity. Christmas is a time of being at home in this way with each other and with God. At Bethlehem God made his home in our human nature and lives amongst us still. He is always at home for us and Christmas is the time when most come home to him. Some choose never to come while others postpone the coming and an-other Christmas slips away. Others feel too far away and unable to come the whole way on their own. He suggests that such children come as far as they can and he will go to meet them.

For those who are away, coming home is a joy beyond compare. To help a loved one, a friend or a work colleague to come home and to come home to God at Christmas is a gift beyond compare.

Happy home-coming and Christmas blessings.

Holy Family

Mt 2:13-15, 19-23

In several families this will be the weekend of the 'scattering.' Many who made it home for the Christmas must now head off again to other places to which life has called them. Hopefully, the visit to the hearth that reared them will have nurtured what is best within them while the hearts of those left at home will have been enriched by the solidarity which Christmas expresses in so many families.

Christmas and family are intimately linked. Christ came as a member of a human family to enable us to be part of God's family. So the first Sunday after Christmas is Family Sunday. It is not a day for preaching about family, but a day for giving thanks for family, for deepening appreciation of what security and life-long fidelity bring to all our lives, for praising God for the wonder that limited human beings such as ourselves are capable of such commitment in peace and joy. Family must surely be an ever-present miracle, a precious gift of a loving and caring Creator. It must never be taken for granted. Like all precious living things it must be protected and nurtured. It cannot be explained or its value proven. It must be experienced to be appreciated.

To convince the young that family is worth committing oneself to, they must meet living witnesses of the sustenance and nurturance that it can bring rather than hear preachers talk about its importance for society.

May Jesus and the other members of his family, Mary and Joseph, continue the miracle of love in all our families tomorrow.

Second Sunday after Christmas

Jn 1:1-18

Each Christmas is different. Somebody's brainchild changes priorities on the toy market and fortunes are made as children are brainwashed about a new essential for happiness. On the social scene, commercial interests devise new attractions to lure the moneyed from home and family and then peer pressure undermines the centrality to this festive season of relationships and faith. As the heart of Christmas is eroded on so many fronts, the essence of our faith needs to be recalled and proclaimed.

The constant core of our Christmas faith is that Jesus Christ is truly son of Mary and Son of God, truly human and truly divine. Each generation of Christians has striven to express the wonder of this mystery in words and found an echo in the hearts of their contemporaries. In this way the great creeds and Glorias came to be written and they handed on the faith from one generation to the next. Writing about such an extraordinary outpouring of God's love, was no task for the faint-hearted. Not only was it impossible to fully describe such a mystery in human language at any time, but words themselves changed their meaning over the years.

Despite these difficulties, the introduction to John's gospel which we read today, has been the never failing well from which faith was nourished over the centuries. Stressing that the Son, the Word as he calls him, has lived from all eternity with the Father, John leads us into the wonder of his becoming flesh and coming among us with the reassuring promise that all who are willing to receive the Word made flesh into their lives, thereby become children of God themselves.

This is the source of all our hope. It is the foundation on which we must build our lives and our world. Happy New Year.

Epiphany

Mt 2:1-12

Natural disasters, famines and wars often awaken a generous willingness in people to do something to alleviate the distress. Close contact with people who care for others in need can cause stirrings of conscience in many people. Sometimes an inexplicable impulse to search for new vistas in life awakens in our hearts. Very often nothing comes of these inspirations. They are crowded over by the concerns and distractions of everyday living and we continue our mediocre humdrum life styles.

The wise men from the East followed another option. They listened to an inner divinely inspired voice inviting them to search for a new presence of their creator among his people. Their courage and tenacity led them to Bethlehem and to Jesus. They were able to bring the good news of the birth of a divine king back to their own people.

A similar opportunity is ours everytime we sense an impulse to goodness or greatness in our hearts. The easy option is to ignore it, knowing that the pressures of life will quickly crowd it out. To follow that route is to live an impoverished life forever. The alternative is to be ever alert to the inspirational moments of our lives and to follow our star with courage, determination and joy. It will lead to similar fulfilment for us as it did for the wise men from the East.

Baptism of the Lord

Mt 3:13-17

Happiness is much sought after. Most people long for it. Many hope they will achieve it. This is the crunch point. Happiness is never the reward of achievement itself even though the development of our full potential in any sphere can bring a great sense of fulfilment. But happiness is something more. It is a gift freely given by God to those open to receive it. Happiness is knowing in the depths of one's being that one is truly loved by God because one is loveable and is capable of responding to that love by loving others. Living out of that radical conviction in everything one does and says is the key route to happiness.

Today's gospel shows us Jesus growing in an awareness of his relationship with the Father. He submitted himself to the ministry of John baptising in the Jordan because that was the Father's will. He was readying himself to receive the full outpouring of the Holy Spirit. Each time we choose the generous option rather than the selfish one, God's will rather than our own, we too are readying ourselves to be filled with the spirit of God, the source of true holiness which is the foundation of all happiness.

Ash Wednesday

Mt 6:1-6, 16-18

When driving, I had grown careless about the use of the car seat-belt. It was not that I doubted its value. It was that my decision to wear it had been corroded through thoughtlessness. Then the *Cork Examiner* reported the prosecutions for not wearing seat belts. Suddenly, I was alerted again to my need for safety. It is not that I fear prosecution but that I appreciate life and good health more.

Lent has the same purpose. It alerts us to our need of God. It deepens our appreciation of God's love for us. It invites us to clean away the corrosion of selfishness and to share his love with others as he told us to. Lent is about decisions; deciding how to put God in his proper place; deciding to pray, to be reconciled, to make contact again with God and his Church.

As I fasten my seat belt, I thank God for life. The prosecutions led me to prayer and care. The Lord uses strange ways; prosecutions for one, maybe, a Lenten Retreat for another.

First Sunday of Lent

Mt 4:1-11

He was a very well connected young man. He was a Jew. His Father really controlled the whole show and, as an only son, he shared in the power himself. He was tempted to use it to smooth his own path in life, but he had other standards and values, including deep respect for the uniqueness of each individual, especially the poor, the despised, the sick and the downtrodden.

Rather than take advantage of his power for his own comfort or glory, he was prepared to spend his whole life in bringing a message of love, hope and forgiveness to all people because that was what his Father wanted. Sharing in this way in his Father's plan was the peak of his own happiness.

It came before all else, no matter what the temptation was to take the soft option. On occasion, these temptations were very strong.

One such occasion is recounted in Sunday's gospel when Jesus, the well-connected only Son of God, is tempted to exploit his privileged position in order to assuage his longing for food, fame and finance.

He was able to resist because he had made room for the Spirit of God in his heart through the forty days of fasting.

The selfish temptations facing each of us are identical. Sometimes we defend our little privileges as if they were inalienable rights. Often, people in key employments use their strength for personal advantage rather than for the good of all the community. Is anyone of us free from abusing our position to protect our own patch?

Today's gospel is a reminder that unless we tackle such selfishness head on, our true greatness as children of a loving Father will be irreversibly eroded. The choice is ours.

Second Sunday of Lent

Mt 17:1-9

One of the great uplifts in teaching is to get an unexpected glimpse of talent or giftedness in a young child. The teacher can know the pupils intimately and then one of them surprises everybody with an academic insight, a flash of heroic generosity, a brilliant mimicry or a beautiful drawing. Whatever it happens to be, it shows the onlookers that there is more to this person than meets the eye.

It was something like that for Peter, James and John when they climbed Mount Tabor with the wandering prophet from Nazareth. They knew him to be a fine preacher as well as an up-and-coming miracle worker. But now, there was something more and it was completely unexpected. Jesus revealed himself as Son of God. Jesus is still revealing himself in unexpected ways and not only on mountain tops but in the routine of everyday. To be open to receive such a revealing of the wonder of God, we need to be like the trio and go apart with Jesus. There is a snag. We would like the revelation but are not willing to pay the price of preparing to receive.

Above all else, Lent is about making time to go apart with Jesus in prayer. It does not matter where but it does matter that it be everyday. Today is a good day to do it better. He awaits us.

Third Sunday of Lent

Jn 4:5-42

Do not let this weekend's gospel slip by unnoticed. Read it in advance. Savour it. Ready your heart for it. Together with the gospels for the following two weekends, it opens up ever deepening aspects of the personality of Jesus and his mission among us. To grow in a knowledge of the Lord Jesus is the road to eternal life. Sunday's Eucharist can be an enriching step on that journey.

The setting is straightforward. Jesus is thirsty. The well is deep. He has no bucket but a stranger woman has. She is from a people ostracised by his own people and she is living publicly in an irregular relationship. The stage is set. Like all law-abiding Jews of the time would do, will he shun the woman or will he ask for and accept a drink from her? He does the unexpected and in requesting a drink, he accepts her as a child of God, a person worthy of the deepest respect just like any other human individual.

He then moves to offer her a share in the life of God which he describes as living water. She glimpses the wonder of the moment and dashes off to share it with the neighbours. The disciples were less than enthusiastic about the Master's involvement with the woman of ill repute.

Drawing water was a humdrum part of the Samaritan woman's life. But it was there she met the Saviour of the world. Her first reaction was sceptical but her generous kindness opened the way for Jesus to touch her and change her life and that of her townspeople.

The lessons for our own lives are many.

Fourth Sunday of Lent

Jn 9:1-41

One of the most appealing advertisements for Third World help is one asking for a few pounds to save a person's sight. Apparently, there is an eye disease prevalent in some countries that leaves many people blind but which can be prevented by simple remedies if there are enough resources available. The advertisement is asking us to do what we can to give a person sight for life. It was the same request that the blind man made to Jesus in today's gospel.

Jesus answered the request and more. He gave the man back his sight so that he could see the world about him like the rest of us. But he gave him something more as well. He gave him vision to penetrate the deeper realities, faith to know that Jesus is Son of God, come into this world. Sight enables us to see the obvious things as they are. Vision is the power to see things as God intends them to be. Vision explores ideals, faith, hope, love, mercy, trust and generosity. Such vision is a gift of God, a gift we need individually and as a people. The young thirst for such a gift. We are called to create an atmosphere where they are open to receive it and to respond to it.

Like the blind man, we must ask for this gift again today for the young, for their teachers, for our leaders and for ourselves.

Fifth Sunday of Lent

Jn 11:1-45

For me, one of the lasting joys from years as a teacher is meeting past pupils in different places and situations. As we talk about the memorable events and characters of times past in school, they prod my memory with vivid descriptions of particular students. They remember one as a hard man, another as a great student, another as a good friend, and so on. The description is usually very apt.

In today's gospel, when Mary and Martha wanted Jesus to know that their brother was sick and near to death, the message they sent was: 'The one you love is sick.' Jesus would know that it was his friend Lazarus who was in danger. Yet, knowing it, he allowed him to die and did not turn up until a few days after the funeral. Certainly, Martha felt that Jesus had let them down badly. But not so. Through Lazarus' death and return to life, Mary and Martha had their faith in Jesus strengthened and their friendship with him deepened. Sometimes we feel let down by God and we retreat from his friendship. But things may not be as they appear and we must trust in his friendship.

Friendship with God or with another person is a precious gift. Like all precious things it must be protected and nurtured through trust given and received in times of apparent failure as well as in times of joy.

Passion Sunday

Mt 26:14-27, 66

As an account of human suffering, the passion story of Jesus has lost much of its impact on the human heart. Recent decades have brought us face to face with accounts and pictures of unbounded human cruelty and suffering. The savagery of war is rivalled only by the violence of crime in a spiral of destruction that endangers our world. Pitted over against the visual and emotional impact of such horrendous events, the mere repetition of the story of the sufferings and death of Jesus in today's gospel can pale into insignificance and degenerate into boredom. But, to be bored with the passion story because of its mildness is to miss the point. The core of the story is not to highlight the cruelty of the Jews and the Romans, severe though it be, but rather to recall in faith who suffered and why he went through it all, not only freely but with a sense of genuine fulfilment.

Love was his motive. Love is always a mystery and God's love more so than any other. While we can never fully understand such total self-giving, we can grow in appreciation and begin to imitate it. That is the opportunity of passion time, to allow our coarsened hearts to be touched again by the overwhelming love of Jesus Christ. In busy and distracted lives, it is important to make time for such a change of heart. To fail to do so is to live unenriched by the most stupendous reality this world has ever known.

Good Friday

Jn 18:1-19:42

A young boy watched every day as the sculptor chiselled away at the block of marble until at last the magnificent statue of a horse emerged. While adults complimented the sculptor on the splendid proportions of the work and the perfection of the detail, the young boy was left with a huge unanswered question. How did the sculptor know that the horse was inside the block of marble? It is easy to smile at the foolishness of the question but the fact is that the sculptor recognised a certain potential in the block of marble and trusted his own patient skill to realise that potential. He chiselled away until his dream horse was realised, taking care never to chisel in such a way that the final product would be damaged.

This can be an image of how our God deals with us. He sees our potential for greatness and works at us in a thousand ways to fulfil his dream for us. Sometimes he allows chiselling through pain, suffering or failure but never beyond what we can take. The same Father had a particular dream for his Son. He was to be redeemer of all the world. The price was passion and death. Sometimes, it looked as if the pain was too much at Gethsemane or on Calvary. But not so. The Father realised the Son's potential and supported him through the Spirit.

No matter how grim the suffering or the future seem, the Father has a great dream for us which he will realise just as he did for his Son. Today's message is not to be afraid, I have overcome the world and so can you.

Holy Saturday

Mt 28:1-10

Every week shows that people without hope die in despair. A society without hope degenerates into fear and violence. Who can help us to overcome the hopelessness of our time and restore joy to the human heart?

Only the person who is prepared to light a candle of goodness at every opportunity rather than curse the darkness of evil. Only the person who daily takes that first small step in building a chain of goodness. Only the person who believes that oftentimes a majority for hope is just one individual with faith and courage. Only the person who knows it is in giving away time, energy and even life itself, that one comes to experience lasting love, human and divine. It is only such a person that can create new life and joy in today's world. The greatest exemplar of such living and leadership is the Lord Jesus whose Resurrection we celebrate this Easter.

Sacrificing all for his brothers and sisters, Calvary seemed to be the end. But the Father in whom he trusted raised him up through the Holy Spirit. A similar transformation awaits each of us. It is not just that we will be raised to life after death, important though that be, but we are enabled by the same Spirit to keep hope alive in the hearts of those whose lives we serve. To be sustained for such a glorious calling, we must fully belong to a community who celebrate faith through prayer, Eucharist and service.

Easter is a time to own our faith and to share it in a way that nurtures hope and evokes joy. Alleluia.

Easter Sunday

Jn 20:1-9

When I was a young boy, there was great excitement when a man I knew well became Lord Mayor of Cork. One day, he was a customer at the counter, the next day he was Cork's first citizen. Suddenly, he was treated just a little differently. Some were delighted. Others resented it. Nobody ignored it. Everybody will have a similar experience. Maybe, it was a foreman becoming a manager, a T.D. becoming a Taoiseach, a priest becoming a bishop. Or, it may just have been the girl you admired getting married. One event can change attitudes significantly.

This happened to Christ. Some saw him as a wandering preacher, maybe even as a great miracle worker, but a dead one after Calvary. Others looked to him with the hope of freedom as one to break the Roman oppression. Their hopes were dashed at Calvary.

Then, suddenly the Resurrection happened. He was risen as he said. He had produced the proof that he was God. Everyone had to take sides. Either you rejected the evidence and saw Christ as a fraud, or you accepted the Resurrection and Jesus as God. One cannot accept the Resurrection and reject the teaching of Christ. The Easter message is that believing he is risen, we commit ourselves again to the full gospel.

Second Sunday of Easter

Jn 20:19-31

Thomas was not the unbelieving one really. It was not that he did not want to believe in the Lord's Resurrection but that he foresaw the consequences. While Peter and the others were overjoyed at the Master's return, Thomas realised that if he were really risen, the consequences were enormous and he was not ready for them. The Resurrection would mean that Jesus was who he claimed to be, the Son of God and not just a prophet. Thomas was holding tough. There was no room for pussy-footing now. Either Jesus was God or he was not. There could be no in-between. Thomas wanted to be sure that Jesus was truly risen. He got what he wanted then, he gave himself totally to the Lord. His decision for Jesus determined the course of the rest of his life.

Something similar happens in our lives. It may be less dramatic and happen gradually over years but the decision is the same. By default, or by decision, each person chooses to believe that Jesus is God, or that he is not, and lives accordingly. To be able to take the faith option is a gift from God. It is a gift to be protected, nurtured and shared. It is to be fully lived or it dies. Middle-of-the-road people are carried by the crowd whichever way it happens to be going and faith is too personal to thrive in that atmosphere. Daily prayer and service nourish this faith and Sunday Eucharist celebrates the belief that Jesus is the risen Lord.

Third Sunday of Easter

Lk 24:13-35

Driving alone gives opportunities to pick up some person looking for a lift. However, each time the situation arises, there usually seems to be good reason to drive past. The old man is standing in too dangerous a place to stop. Such young children
should not be encouraged to hitch. The hiker's back-pack looks
very awkward. Maybe that fellow is a bank robber, a terrorist, a
con man or just plain lazy.

Yet, each time I overcome such negative reactions and give
somebody a lift, both of us are enriched. Almost always a life
story is shared. It may be a story of illness, romance, work or unemployment as the passenger turns out to be visiting a hospital,
going on a date, racing for work or searching for a job. Each one
gives me another insight into life and into how God touches our
lives.

As we hear in Sunday's gospel, something similar happened to
the two disciples on the road to Emmaus as they fled Jerusalem
in disappointment and fear. They allowed Jesus to join them
and, at journey's end, they shared their supper with him without knowing who he was. Their reward was great. They met the
Risen Lord.

All life is a journey, much of it lived in disappointments and
fears that entrap us into privacy and self-centredness. But when
we are not blinded by our own preoccupations and share life's
journey in faith with those around us, love can be enkindled in
our hearts and we, too, can meet the Risen Lord in our fellow
travellers.

God's gift of his presence comes to us through one another. It is
a gift that can fill our hearts with joy this Easter time.

Fourth Sunday of Easter

Jn 10:1-10

It is the time of year when students wonder where the school year has gone so quickly. Examinations are on the horizon and lost opportunities cannot be recalled. In some hearts there are vague recriminations that if the year were on offer again, it would be put to better use. But it is not on offer again. Some opportunities do not repeat themselves. In a sense, we have to make our opportunities and make the most of them. We are responsible for the use we choose to make of what life offers each one of us.

Today's liturgy is set aside as a reminder of a particular opportunity offered to those called to priesthood and religious life. It is a privileged opportunity of friendship with the Lord through his service and service to his people. It is offered to those whom God chooses for his own reasons. Like all opportunities it carries its own responsibilities. It is an opportunity that some accept and that others refuse or let slip away. Vocations Sunday is a day to pray especially for those whom the Lord is calling today to his full-time service, that they may seize with Spirit-filled joy the opportunity that is on offer for the one life they have.

Imagine how much poorer our world would be if Mother Teresa, Pope John Paul, St Francis and thousands of others had not listened to and responded fully to God's call to them. So, in one way or another, Vocations Sunday is everybody's business.

Fifth Sunday of Easter

Jn 14:1-12

It is really hard to imagine that anybody could treasure each of his friends in a unique way without comparing one with the other. Our lives are filled with comparisons and competition. It starts with the Baby Shows rating the bonny toddlers, first, second and third. It ends with funeral caskets and the wreaths. In between there are the endless comparisons of talent, skill, success, wealth, breeding, power, usefulness, status and even holiness. Snobbery pervades the fibre of our society.

It all seems so contradictory for a people who are made in the image of God. To help us to appreciate that with our God there are no such comparisons, Jesus told us that in his Father's house there are many rooms, an individual place for each one of us. With him, there are no comparisons. He treasures each equally as a friend. When we believe that, we can trust in God and accept that Jesus is gone before us to prepare that place for us. He is truly the way to peaceful happiness.

Sixth Sunday of Easter

Jn 14:15-21

May is a superb month for hill and mountain walking. The improving weather, the stretch in the evenings, the budding trees, the blossoming wild flowers, the chorus of the breeding birds all entice one out of doors and into the wild. A guidebook is invaluable on such trips but more valuable still is a congenial, well informed guide. Such a guide knows not only the essentials but the enrichments and is one whose interest is as much in companionship as in the peak to be climbed. For this guide, experienced knowledge is a gift shared generously rather than doled out arrogantly. On the mountain trail, such a fellow traveller is a precious godsend. On the journey through life, such a companion is a blessing beyond compare.

Sunday's gospel tells us of Jesus promising each one of us that we can have such a one always at our side. He promises to send as advocate the Spirit of the living God. The core of the promise is that the Spirit of God will live within oneself but this Spirit lives also in each friend, neighbour, spouse, workmate and it is often through their actions and inspiration that we become aware of this helper touching our lives and forming our hearts. This Spirit advocate enables each one to achieve the fullness of her or his potential and to joyfully appreciate one's giftedness.

Such an advocate lives in us for ourselves and for one another. We need to hear his voice and to respond today.

The Ascension of the Lord

Mt 28:16-20

Friendship is one of life's greatest blessings. It is both simple and mysterious. In a myriad of ways, it can begin so casually between neighbours, between work and sporting colleagues, as well as between people committed to similar ideas. The link of shared values and common interests is the seed that sometimes develops into a bond of mutual friendship. It is a mystery why some connections blossom into precious personal relationships and others do not. All friendship is enriched by mutual concern, care and celebration. But the refining fire that fashions friendship into ongoing and lifegiving relationship is crisis and difficulty, shared and survived. The friend who stands by one in the darkest moments of trouble is the true friend for whom we all long and treasure always.

Before Jesus left his disciples to return to the Father, he promised them such enduring friendship. He was sending them to baptise all peoples, so founding his church worldwide. To sustain them and their successors in their daunting task, he gave them an unconditional guarantee that he would be with them no matter what crisis hit his church. In our time, it is a reassuring promise. It is the promise of this Ascension Day.

Seventh Sunday of Easter

Jn 17:1-11

In every friendship, there comes a time when the realisation dawns that there is more to this relationship than convenience, that there is a bond, an appreciation of the other's uniqueness, a sharing of life, love and hopes. In Sunday's gospel, the prayer of Jesus shows his awareness of such a critical point in his relationship with his disciples and their relationship with the Father through him. As the foreboding days of the passion and death loomed ahead of him, Jesus was anxious for himself and for his followers. Conscious that his life's work was nearly over, he entrusted his disciples back to the Father. His prayer for them was that they would always believe that he was the Son of God and that in living out that belief, they would make present in every relationship the love that he had brought to the world.

These times are no less ominous for us individually and as a people. At home and abroad, violence, poverty, selfishness, fear, despondency, hopelessness stalk the land. But Jesus entrusts us, too, to the Father to whom we truly belong. With such an assurance in our heart we can never lose hope. Rather, our calling in the world is to keep hope alive, a hope built on an appreciation that we belong to the Father no matter what our troubles or our failures and that he will care for us always. Sunday's Eucharist nourishes that hope within us.

Pentecost

Jn 20:19-23

A mother's birthday has a special appeal. It usually evokes a significant response in family members, especially in the strays and in the black sheep. There is an awareness of the life she has given and nurtured. The blessings she has bestowed are remembered at least fleetingly. The opportunities she has created are often recalled with joy. The chances bungled are cloaked in resentment or forgiveness. There is gratitude for the past even if there is now a realisation that she was not as perfect as was once thought. Overall, there is a recognition that the bonds between a mother and those she has formed rarely die totally, no matter how they may be neglected.

Pentecost Sunday is the birthday of our faith mother, the church. At Pentecost, we celebrate the coming of the Holy Spirit on the disciples to begin a new life between them, a life that bound them together as a community of believers who sustain each other in respect-filled hope and generous service and who, through that shared faith, make God's love present in the world for succeeding generations.

From this mother, we have all received life and grace. Her begetting and her nurturance have been experienced in a myriad of ways by different people. This mother has cradled saints and forgiven sinners. She has inspired heroism and battled against selfishness. She has been served by the faithful and manipulated by the ambitious. She has been trusted by the poor and exploited by the powerful. Through it all, she has kept faith in Jesus alive over the centuries and handed on to us Baptism, Reconciliation and Eucharist despite persecution, sin and failure. This achievement shows that God is truly with her and lives within her.

This weekend we salute you, mother church. We claim you, own you and return to you. We rejoice on your birthday and hope that all the family make contact soon, especially those who have been away.

Trinity Sunday

Jn 3:16-18

The four-year-old took me aback when she told me that even though her mother was very good, she often made mistakes. For whatever reason, the sophisticated youngster's implicit trust in a caring parent is already tottering. The loss is great. Humanly, we are made for trusting relationships. In the adult world, every time trust is undermined, we are all diminished. Trust can be misplaced and even well-placed trust can be undermined. Coping with such betrayal stretches maturity and love. Some cope by not risking trust again with anybody and so retreat into an impoverished self-centred lifestyle. Others are secure enough within themselves to absorb the pain and reach out again in trusting friendship, believing that we are called to a greatness beyond our limited human vision.

Such people have glimpsed into the heart of God. What makes God God is that he remains always faithful to us. No matter what our betrayal, he continues to trust us again and again and to call us forward to the greatness he has destined for us. This greatness is to share the inner love life of God, where Father, Son and Spirit live in an eternal bond that we call the Blessed Trinity.

This trust-filled relationship is beyond our understanding but it is open to our experience, appreciation and imitation. We experience it every time we return to God in our failure and sin to accept the healing touch of his reconciling love. We appreciate it in the quietness of reflective prayer, especially in the eucharistic presence.

Our imitation shows itself when our brothers and sisters find in us a forgiving heart that harbours no resentment but allows the powerful love of God permeate every relationship.

Corpus Christi

Jn 6:51-58

Memory is often very selective. No two people remember a particular event in quite the same way. Certainly, the victors and the vanquished will have very different memories of the crucial moments in a sporting encounter. But even when all the participants agree on the actual happenings, the full significance of some aspects of an event will only dawn on people as time goes by. Something like that happened to the disciples as they recalled the Last Supper. The highlight obviously was the gift to the young church of the Lord's Body and Blood in the Eucharist. It is the foundation and nourishment of our faith. Without Eucharist, there can be no church of Jesus Christ. The first disciples recognised the central importance of the Lord's command to break Eucharistic bread in memory of him forever. But gradually, they remembered another experience of that remarkable evening and this is the one recorded in John's gospel years later. It tells how Jesus washed their feet, a service done only by a slave in their culture and he challenged them to serve each other in a similar way.

So Christ's farewell twin gifts to the world were the Eucharist and a community of followers who would serve those in need until the end of time. Today, we are asked to make the same gifts present to a world that is more receptive to actions than to words, to service than to mystery, to witnesses than to preachers. It is only when people have experienced unconditional love and service from the followers of Jesus that they will seek out the source of such love in the Eucharist. 'I have given you an example so that you may copy what I have done to you.'

Second Sunday in Ordinary Time

Jn 1:29-34

On a cold January day, standing in the rain in the innermost reaches of the forest at Gougane Barra, it was hard to visualise that the little rivulets forming before one's eyes were the source of the river Lee. From this small beginning, the river gathers strength, carves out a valley route, generates electricity, harbours salmon, supplies water to towns and city, creates the port of Cork and generally nurtures life as it flows seawards. From this apparently insignificant beginning, a river is born that enriches so many lives, most of whom never advert to its presence.

Something similar happens in every Christian life. A seed is planted in love. A child is born. Rivulets of faith coalesce to tune a heart to hear God's call. A generous if tentative response prepares the way for a deeper call and a more courageous response. Sometimes the call is not heeded and a stream of goodness dries up. But God is a persistent lover who never ceases to issue new calls and new invitations. No matter how insignificant or how late, it may seem to be, each answered call of God can be a wellspring of faith and love touching many hearts as the years roll by.

Today's gospel recounts how John the Baptist, in fulfilling his own life role, came to recognise the Chosen One of God and then was led to martyrdom, but not before he had pointed out the Messiah to Andrew and John, the first disciples. Our pattern of life vocation is the same. Through daily fidelity, we recognise Jesus and point him out to those who do not know him so that together we may become a stream of peace and goodness enriching the world of our time.

Third Sunday in Ordinary Time

Mt 4:12-23

The arrest of an innocent family member must send a chill down the spine of every member of the wider family circle. The anxiety is that innocence may not win out over power. The natural reaction is to retreat to where one feels most secure. This is exactly what Jesus did when he heard that cousin John had been arrested. He knew that the Baptist was an upright man whose only crime was to have denounced the misdeeds of the powerful. But he knew too that the treacherous Herod controlled the security forces, so he retreated to Galilee, the home province. He settled in Capernaum rather than the home village of Nazareth. This change of residence was significant. He had cut the ties with home and had to be about the Father's business of proclaiming the good news. This meant that he must go where the Spirit led him. As we read in Sunday's first reading, it had been foretold that the oppressed people of Zebulon and Naphtali would one day experience a great light when a saviour came among them. This day had arrived with the coming of Jesus to Capernaum.

The core of his message, then as now, was amazingly simple. God is very close to us. He is indeed, within us. He is in everybody who touches our lives. An awareness of God's presence at every hand's turn is the beginning of holiness. Sin is the stifling of such awareness. Repentance is the willingness to let God into the little details of our daily lives. Sunday's message is repent, for the kingdom of God is close at hand.

Fourth Sunday in Ordinary Time

Mt 5:1-12

Governments are often elected on promises rather than performance. In recessionary times, the key promise is usually to narrow the gap between the haves and the have-nots. It seems to be a daunting task.

Some say it cannot be done, but for many people innovative government action and leadership seems to be their only hope of a job, a place to live or adequate medical care. Creative policy statements are a start but it is their implementation that makes a difference. Goodwill without decisive action is sterile.

Sunday's gospel is the most revolutionary social policy statement every produced. It is revolutionary because it turns this world's value systems upside down. It suggests that the gentle will possess the earth but our experience indicates that it is the powerful who grab the perks while the gentle powerless go without.

Jesus wants to make us aware of another way of living. It is the experience of living generosity rather than selfishness, of practising forgiveness rather than revenge, of hungering for what is right rather than for what benefits oneself, of seeing others as children of the same loving Father rather than people to be used.

It is the policy life statement for followers of Jesus. We are judged by how we live it. Our living it is some people's only chance of a decent life or indeed of life at all.

We are called to heroic generosity and courage today. He is always with us.

Fifth Sunday in Ordinary Time

Mt 5:13-16

I stayed on talking to Annie when Mary and John left. 'They are the salt of the earth', she said as they closed the door. Now in her eighties, Annie lives alone, in poor health. She has no relatives and most of the old neighbours have died or moved away. Mary is in a bedsitter next door. John is her boyfriend. In their early twenties, they hope to marry in the Summer. To Annie, they are as good as any son and daughter. They shop for her, wash and clean. She even shares their supper occasionally before they go to a disco. From her bed she shares their secrets, their hopes, their struggle to get a home together.

For Annie they are the light of her world. Through them she sees her God. The light of their love keeps her hope alive. Their daily visits are the salt that adds flavour to her life.

At today's Mass we are asked to share our bread with the hungry, to bring relief to the oppressed, to be the salt of the earth and the light of the world. Mary and John have found one way of doing it.

Sixth Sunday in Ordinary Time

Mt 5:17-37

Sometimes a gospel passage has so many varied aspects that different points strike different individuals as the key message. Sunday's gospel is one such passage. It ranges from anger to adultery, from scandal to swearing, from insincerity to integrity. But despite the variation, the core message is clear. Only the person who continues to grow into the fullness of the law of love of God and of the neighbour can join in the friendship of God now and forever.

A common danger for us is to bargain with God's law, to play one part off another. To accept that one should not kill seems equitable enough but to always refrain from denigrating another's character seems above and beyond what is humanly reasonable. If we abide by the precept of avoiding murder, we can fool ourselves into believing that character assassination is not too bad after all. Such skin deep virtue evokes Christ's unequivocal denunciation.

He says clearly that he is calling us to a better way, to a higher ideal, a more generous response. True, we will fail. He knows that and his forgiveness is always available. But his challenge is never to settle for mediocrity, to respond daily to the seeds of courageous faith he sows in our hearts, to be willing to let him change us every year of our lives. It is a glorious calling.

Seventh Sunday in Ordinary Time

Mt 5:38-48

In all negotiations, the talented, the strong, the entrenched, the hard-working argue that they deserve more because of their contributions to the world around them. On the other hand, the poor, the less able, the unemployed can only highlight their needs. The latter's case may not be heard but it is irrefutable. Every human person needs food, shelter, clothing, health care and the opportunity to live with dignity. Needs are always more important than desserts. We are stewards of our talents, not owners. Our strengths must flower in gentleness.

Fortunately God always gives us what we need rather than what we deserve. We need his merciful forgiveness for our failure to live with an appreciation that all good things are his gifts to all humankind. His forgiveness is given to all whether we deserve it or not. Today's gospel invites us to follow that example, to be always first movers in forgiveness, to be generous beyond measure in being reconciled to the one who has wronged us. Only God can help us to do so daily. He will.

Eighth Sunday in Ordinary Time

Mt 6:24-34

Our weather is a constant topic of conversation. In waiting rooms, the seasonableness of the day is a good ice-breaker among strangers. In public houses, the changing weather is a safer topic than politics for the newcomer. Such pervasive weather talk reminds us of how deeply our work, recreation, health and well-being are influenced by the vagaries of our climate. We partially protect ourselves from its worst ravages but we really cannot change it.

So we experience coping with aspects of life which are beyond our control. Indeed, in all areas of life, much more seems to happen by chance than by human design. People cope with this lack of control over events in different ways. Some worry endlessly about how to provide for every contingency. At the other end of the spectrum, there are people who make no provisions and leave everything to chance.

In between are the majority who, in our time, tend to be over anxious and over security conscious. For this majority, today's gospel has a clear message. Do not waste you energy or lose your peace by worrying. It serves no purpose. Instead, trust your God, in whose hands the world safely rests. We are creatures lovingly in his care.

Instead of dissipating our energy on worrying, the advice is to focus it on being loved and loving. It is a happy alternative.

Ninth Sunday in Ordinary Time

Mt 7:21-27

Most of us take foundations for granted. They are usually completely hidden and we do not expect them to impinge on us directly. To discover a defect in the foundations of one's house must be a traumatic experience for a home owner. Defective foundations may be due to a geological fault, poor materials or incompetent construction, but the resulting shock is the same no matter what the cause. The sense of alarm can be akin to a sense of betrayal. We rely so totally on foundations that their failure to match expectations often undermines our sense of well being and security. This personal distress can be even more devastating when the foundations involved are not of our homes but our whole way of life.

This is why Jesus warns us to build our lives upon rock, the rock of truth, of belief in him and in his gospel, the rock of faith, hope and love. Such building can be very challenging. The easier option is to build on the sands of selfishness and self interest, of money and comfort. Choosing this option is a recipe for disaster. Unlike house foundations, we are constantly consolidating or undermining the fundamental values of our lives. Indeed, life style betrays the calibre of personal foundations. Today's gospel is an invitation to examine our basic attitudes to daily living and a challenge to align them with the values of Christ. It is a gospel value we ignore at our peril.

Tenth Sunday in Ordinary Time

Mt 9:9-13

Catholics are often classified as practising or non-practising. For the former, today's gospel could be disconcerting. For the latter, it could have a great message of hope. In the gospels, lapsed Jews were described as sinners and it is with them that we find Jesus sharing Levi's going away party as he leaves tax-collecting to go into fulltime ministry. No respectable rabbi should risk fraternising with these social outcasts but Jesus did. Such conduct did not endear him to those who saw themselves as faithful to the law of Moses and its customary rituals. Their self-righteousness irked Jesus. With a somewhat severe directness, he reminded them that an essential prerequisite to receiving God is to acknowledge our sinfulness and our need of him. Only those who know their need of love, can be truly loved.

Our goodness is not our own handiwork. It is pure gift given through the mercy of God. Such mercy is our hope. Such mercy must inspire all in pastoral ministry to give priority time and resources to the lapsed, the deprived, prisoners, social rejects. Jesus did.

Eleventh Sunday in Ordinary Time

Mt 9:36-10:8

June is peak season for ordinations to the priesthood. Throughout Ireland men will have hands laid upon them by a bishop in the age old ceremony that empowers them to celebrate the Eucharist, to reconcile humankind to God and to anoint the sick. As well as baptising, preaching and teaching the gospel, these men are called to build up praying communities of believers who make justice, forgiveness and love present in the world through lives of committed caring service to those most in need. It is a noble calling especially in these times when the odds seemed stacked against anyone trying to live out the values of Jesus. But things were not better in the world when Jesus called the original twelve, as we hear in today's gospel. Paganism supported by the power of the Roman empire was rampant all around them. The religious leaders of the time had succumbed to the civil oppressors. The twelve were ill-equipped for the task entrusted to them. But they believed that Jesus had called them and would not fail them.

In today's bewildered world, Jesus still calls Andrews, Johns, Peters, Patricks and others to whom he entrusts the same task as he did to the original twelve. May all whom he calls, answer. There will never be a better time to do so than now.

Twelfth Sunday in Ordinary Time

Mt 10:26-33

As never before, winners evoke admiration and allegiance. World record-breakers command enormous sponsorship fees. Olympic champions have become household names. It seems that everyone loves a winner and wants to be identified with success. Such adulation is enjoyable and harmless enough but in the serious business of daily living, the one who died on the cross demands that his followers stand by him on Calvary as well as at Cana, in Gethsemane as in Galilee, on Good Friday as well as on Palm Sunday. There is never enough room on a band-wagon and so he has no shortage of fair weather friends. But today's gospel is very clear. Jesus expects friends to be courageous as well as compassionate, committed as well as concerned when called upon to promote and defend the values of truth and justice for which he lived and died. He asks us for a deepening loyalty in response to his own unswerving fidelity to us. Martyrdom may be the result but his care will overcome all our trials.

Thirteenth Sunday in Ordinary Time

Mt 10:37-42

Joe's comment on what I had written was brief and telling. 'All challenge and no comfort.' At times it could well have been the attitude of Jesus towards his Father's will. After all, that will led him to have no place to lay his head, to be driven out of his home town of Nazareth and eventually to take up his cross and be crucified. In doing the Father's will, there was certainly challenge for Jesus as there will be for us. Yet, as today's gospel reminds us, there is no other way for a Christian to live, no other way to receive God's love. 'Anyone who does not take up his cross and follow in my footsteps is not worthy of me.'

Doing God's will brings pain, power and peace. The pain is eased when we realise that good is only done at great cost to those who do it. There is no such thing as cheap love. The power comes from God who is always with us so that every obstacle can be overcome. There is no need to fear our weakness. Peace is a gift of God, a joy, a happiness. There is no peace to match the peace that comes from doing God's will, from taking up our daily cross. It is a peace that nothing can upset or touch. It is the peace of God's friendship that makes all cross-bearing worthwhile. It is only through living the challenge that we can experience the comfort.

Fourteenth Sunday in Ordinary Time

Mt 11:25-30

TV coverage of the World Cup was a wonderful scientific achievement, linking people worldwide with the event simultaneously. Barriers of distance, oceans, mountains and national boundaries were overcome as the pictures were relayed to satellite and beamed back into homes across the planet. Interest and technological expertise united millions of people of many races, colours and creeds. Hopefully, this linkup will lead to a better understanding between peoples and anything that improves mutual acceptance is to be encouraged.

But despite such linkups, our world is a divided and violent one with dissension not only between countries but within countries and within families. Despite being created as one human family, we continue to live as islands of fear and selfishness. The barrier that renders us unwilling or unable to reach out trustfully to one another is an attitude of mind and heart that sees might as right when power and privilege are on our side.

No technology can overcome this barrier. Only the Spirit of God, present in our world through us, can accomplish this task. This Spirit shows itself in sincerity rather than self-righteousness, in simplicity rather than success, in reverence rather than rejection, in acceptance rather than achievement. Reverence is strength built on faith. Gentleness is strength founded on love.

Such gentleness was at the core of the life and teaching of Jesus as we hear in today's gospel.

Fifteenth Sunday in Ordinary Time

Mt 13:1-23

Reading this weekend's gospel while seated on a rocky perch overlooking sun-drenched Killarney sends mind and heart racing in several directions at once. The magnificent scenery evokes wonder, joy, contentment, praise and thanks to the creator of all. The lakes, mountains and luxuriant growth in purples, yellows, whites, reds, blues and so many shades of green are breathtaking. The abundant growth of limestone soil is nurtured by abundant rainfall and mild winters. Yet, here too, there are oppressors and casualties, aggressors and victims. Even in the most environmentally friendly areas, some plants lose their space, light and food and so they die. In several places, the rampaging rhododendrons advance relentlessly and crowd out a myriad of less aggressive shrubs and wildlife.

The gospel parable echoes within me with its message of seed and sower, of root and rock, of thorn and triumph, of failure and fruitfulness. Jesus alerts his followers to the fact that even the powerful seedling of his love can be choked to death by the thorns of selfishness and security, of pleasure and popularity, of comfort and compromise. We need to make daily space in our lives for the word of God to take root in our hearts. We may be too busy or too distracted to receive the gift for which we are created. But we have the assurance of the Lord that the fertile seed of our goodness, which he plants in the rich soil of our hearts, will bear fruit a hundredfold, if only we give it a chance. The choice is between thorns of frustration and a harvest of love.

Sixteenth Sunday in Ordinary Time

Mt 13:24-43

Advertising is constantly alerting farmers to new and high-pow-ered chemical ways of eliminating weeds from among their crops. Today's gospel seems to have Jesus advocating a different policy. He suggests that the darnel be allowed to grow along with the wheat until harvest time.

Of course, Jesus was not giving agricultural advice but using a familiar everyday image to make a point. At that time the only way of eliminating weeds was to pull them up one by one and that obviously endangered the wheat crop itself.

This was especially true in the very dry climate of Palestine where every disturbance of the soil led to the evaporation of pre-cious moisture. So on balance, it was better to give the whole field a chance until the harvest and Jesus had confidence that the wheat crop would win out.

Jesus' message was a very personal one. Within each of us there is a mixture of goodness and selfishness. We struggle to develop the better side and to curb our weaknesses. It will be so until we die. God allows it that way.

He invites us to produce a great harvest of generosity towards others, even though we fail in a thousand ways. He has great confidence in the seed of love that he has planted in us at baptism. It will win out.

At the harvest time of death, it is the power of his love that will burn out all trace of evil and ready us to live in his presence for-ever. Today's message is not one of judgement but of encourage-ment. God trusts us.

Seventeenth Sunday in Ordinary Time

Mt:13:44-52

Challenging times face the young. Opportunities for new exciting experiences are part of their lifestyle. Travel, study, music, sport, service, technology, religious exploration and the relationship revolution all have the potential to enrich young lives. Lack of jobs, manipulative pressure, uncertainty about values, changing attitudes to faith and family, absence of engaging role-models, and substance abuse endanger the core of human maturity and happiness. Choices facing the young today are stark with life-long consequences stretching into eternity. It is in these choices that the young must find God. Finding always implies a willingness to search.

In our rapidly changing world, many modern options were not experienced previously so this generation must pathfind its life routes without traditional life maps. Past conventions on their own are an inadequate foundation for living present day commitments. But faith and fidelity, truth and trust, family and forgiveness, integrity and idealism, endurance and example, sensitivity and service are as essential now as they ever were. It is through living out these values daily that the pearl of great price of this weekend's gospel is found. There is no other way. Searching for a fix for instant happiness is futile. Cheap offers of fulfilment are not bargains. The real treasure is believing that one is made for permanent love, giving it and receiving it from God and from one another, and living accordingly. It is the one thing worth giving one's life to. To enable the young to search and find this treasure is the challenge facing all of us today.

Eighteenth Sunday in Ordinary Time

Mt 14:13-21

It happened in Christ's time and it has happened often since. When Jesus asked the disciples to feed the hungry crowd, their first reaction was to point out the difficulties. The little food they had would make so little difference to the throngs and there was no point in even making a start. Their answer was to send the people away and to let others care for them. Jesus would not accept that viewpoint. He prodded them into sharing even the little they had and he multiplied it a thousandfold.

These first disciples were paralysed by the apparent hopelessness of the situation. They saw only the difficulties, whereas Jesus was opening up an opportunity.

In our time, the hungry of the Third World or the homeless of our own country, the increased number of reluctant emigrants or the huge number of unemployed, the growth of alcoholism among the young or the disintegration of family life, the decline in religious practice or the undermining of moral values, all present situations so discouraging that we may fail to make whatever little contribution we can to building a better world, making God's kingdom come. Such paralysis is unworthy of a follower of Jesus.

Today's gospel is a call to be especially aware of the little opportunities where we can enrich even one of our brothers and sisters and to realise that God will bless our efforts beyond all our expectations. Trust him and let him prod you into action.

Nineteenth Sunday in Ordinary Time

Mt 14:22-33

Life is a tough haul for many people some of the time and for some people most of the time. This is particularly true for committed people trying to live out Christian values in everyday living. At times, they feel that having been baptised, confirmed and perhaps married or ordained, they set out in life alone into the headwinds of poverty and pain, unemployment and unscrupulosity, injustice and infidelity, loneliness and limitation. They are unable to make much progress. The church may be there some place in the background praying, but it does not seem to be in the thick of the gale of life.

In the gospel story this weekend, the disciples find themselves in a similar scenario. The master goes praying in the safety of the hills while they are crossing the sea of Galilee in the teeth of a storm. They are not making much progress. But the Master is at hand and ready to help when asked. It seems that he would have passed by if Peter had not called out.

Maybe we need to invite him into our lives more realistically, not confining him to our church-going and its related activities but seeking his wisdom, courage, guidance and help in everyday situations. It is help he will give through one another, through a good Christian neighbour or group, through strength to carry on until a better day comes. What is true is that his coming is as certain as the dawn, no matter how troubled the sea of life is.

Twentieth Sunday in Ordinary Time

Mt 15:21-28

At all times and in most places there are people who find them-selves on the edge, who do not quite belong, who do not get their share, who are deprived and in need. In our time, there are people like the homeless, the handicapped, the travellers, the unemployed and the uneducated who feel outside the main stream of our society and are often marginalised.

In Christ's time, the Canaanites were one of the marginalised groupings. As descendants of a pagan tribe of doubtful morals, they were utterly despised by the Jews. So when a Caananite woman came to the true Jew, Christ, to heal her daughter, she knew that she was reaching across the great divide. The recep-tion she got at first did not encourage her but she persevered. Somehow, she sensed that there was more to Christ than inherit-ed prejudices against her people. In her heart, she knew that he cared for her sick child. As we read in today's gospel, her trust was not misplaced and Christ cared for her daughter.

In our time, the brave reach out for justice for the marginalised. They hope that under the current malaise of greed and grasping there is a Christlike generosity. May their courage on behalf of the needy, and their trust in the better off, always evoke a re-sponse worthy of followers of Christ.

Twenty-first Sunday in Ordinary Time

Mt 16:13-20

Personal identity is crucial to happiness and wellbeing. Coming to a knowledge of who one is can be a lifetime task, but it is important to be searching in the right direction. Others create an identity for us based on our achievements and our possessions or, indeed, on our failures and our poverty. Some are seen to have made it while others are written off because they have not done so and are not likely to. Such criteria of identity are particularly destructive when one applies them to oneself or to those one loves. Possessions are very transient while achievements are often only targets for others to surpass.

Our true identity has a more solid foundation. It is based on the fact that we are children of God, created in his image, with a role in life that no other can fulfil. To really know this in one's heart, to live accordingly and to be able to share it with others is the peak of human destiny and is the road to unending happiness and love. God gradually leads us along that road if we are willing to heed the Spirit living in our hearts and in our relationships.

It was by such powerful listening that Jesus came to a fuller realisation of his own identity as Son of God and son of Mary, as human and divine.

Others saw him as a great miracle worker or even as a prophet back from the dead but, as we read in this weekend's gospel, Peter was inspired to recognise Jesus for who he really was and to realise who he was himself in relation to Jesus. It is a gift that will be given to us if we seek it and are open to receive it in this weekend's Eucharist.

Twenty-second Sunday in Ordinary Time

Mt 16:21-27

There is not one of us who would not wish to shield those we love from suffering. The parent is always on the lookout to protect the young from all the human hazards that face every child on the road to maturity. In marriage, the partners try to shelter one another from undue anxiety and distress. To spare a loved-one pain brings a deep fulfilment and joy.

St Peter was no exception. The bond between him and Christ had grown deeper over the previous months so he was horrified when Christ spoke of his future suffering in Jerusalem. Peter would have none of that nonsense. He assured Christ that such talk was out of place. But of course, it was not out of place. In God's plan Christ was to suffer and die on his road to resurrection and glory, on his journey to open up for us the eternal life of God. In his agony, Christ was lonely and afraid but he knew that the Father would not desert him no matter what happened.

The road of suffering is the road of life travelled by many. It is good to know that Christ travelled it despite Peter's protests which we hear in today's gospel. It is reassuring to believe that the Father will never desert us no matter what our agony.

'Father, I surrender myself into your hands without reserve and with confidence beyond all questioning because you are my Father.'

Twenty-third Sunday in Ordinary Time

Mt 18:15-20

The gap between rich and poor widens at every level, not only in our own country but between ourselves and Third World countries. The E.U. accumulates food mountains and millions die of starvation, some even within the E.U. itself. Political institutions are unwilling or unable to redress the situation. Goodwill is strangled by the economic establishment. On many fronts, evil seems to thrive and indeed to have the upper hand. Violence is on the increase. Financial self-protection is the pervasive culture. Self-righteousness is fashionable. Where wrong is condemned, few convince the wrongdoer of the evil of his ways or enable him to make a new beginning. Being the easier option, condemnation has replaced conversion. Of course, conversion is a dangerous process. It frequently demands changes in oneself as well as in the one who has listened to the suggested better option. Conversion of another always involves high risk of rejection because few welcome a challenge to their complacency.

Yet this weekend's gospel is a clarion call to awaken each other's conscience to an awareness of right and wrong and to do it in a way that invites commitment rather than creates alienation. This is the crunch. Condemnation is merely human. Conversion always involves collaboration with the Spirit of God which Jesus assures us will be present where two or three are gathered in his name.

Belonging to and heeding such faith-filled cells will open us to conversion ourselves and enable us to bring it to others.

Twenty-fourth Sunday in Ordinary Time

Mt 18:21-35

Our response to being wronged, to having a precious trust betrayed, to our own failures, is often a mixture of resentment, disappointment, anger, despair, mixed in with a craving for justice and a seedling of forgiveness struggling for survival someplace in our emotionally turbulent hearts. It is vital for our wellbeing that this seedling not only survives but triumphs. Justice is essential, reasonable, arguable and human. Forgiveness is mysterious, exciting, energising, life-giving, painful and divine. It is a response of love.

Punishment concentrates on the evil to be redressed while forgiveness focuses on the love potential of the one who had failed. The difference is in the attitude of mind and heart of the one who is offended. Punishment always has an element of righting the balance. Forgiveness is allowing love to absorb the agony without bitterness. True forgiveness is never conditional or manipulative. Rather it risks its own security to give an offender's goodness another chance.

There are two aspects to forgiveness that are inextricably linked, the willingness to forgive others and the openness to accept forgiveness oneself. Both aspects grow or decline together within each heart. As long as we refuse to even try to forgive another, we become incapable of forgiving ourselves or of allowing another to forgive us. On the other hand, every time we forgive we open ourselves to be filled with peace.

Forgiveness like love is a mystery. It goes beyond justice, apology and retribution. It is appreciated through being experienced. It cannot be measured or counted. Hence, the command of Jesus in this weekend's gospel is to forgive unconditionally again and again so that our hearts may be enriched beyond all understanding.

Twenty-fifth Sunday in Ordinary Time

Mt 20:1-16

On every side, people are more conscious of their rights with less concern for the real needs of others. The unemployed, the homeless, the less fortunate experience themselves more and more excluded by the better off. Those who have want more. Such attitude was there from the beginning, apparently. While Adam and Eve had everything they needed, they were tempted to desire something extra with disastrous consequences. The early workers in the vineyard were not satisfied with their agreed wage and begrudged the latecomers a similar wage.

Today's gospel is a stern reminder to be aware of the destructive selfishness that can so easily take over our hearts. We tend to ignore the fact that we have no claim to this world's goods over and above our brothers and sisters at home or elsewhere. Creation and life itself are God's gifts, given for all equally. Talents and work opportunities are not entitlements to self aggrandisement but rather make one responsible for building a better world for all. No matter how small is the contribution we make to our neighbour's welfare, it is ours to make.

In pointing out how subtle and deep-rooted selfishness is in our hearts, today's gospel is frighteningly challenging but we ignore it at our peril. The antidote to selfishness is generosity. Try it several times daily.

Twenty-sixth Sunday in Ordinary Time

Mt 21:28-32

Joe never attends a planning meeting. He does not see himself as articulate enough to formulate plans for the neighbourhood or for the parish. But when it comes to doing the job he is always there to work. He knows that actions speak louder than words and he lives accordingly. The proof of faith is good works. Love of God is shown above all in generous service to the neighbour in need, without distinction of social class or religious practice. Joe is often impatient with people who promise much but deliver little, who think that talking nice words is an adequate substitute for effective action.

Jesus shared Joe's impatience, as we read in today's gospel, where the father tells his two sons to go to work in his vineyard. One refuses at first but goes. The other promises to go but does not. It is the former who actually does what the father asks and that is what counts. Among the Jews of his own time there were many people who professed their faith in God but refused to live as Jesus taught. On the other hand, there were people who had not lived according to the book but, when invited by Jesus to repent and make a fresh start, they did so enthusiastically. It is these who received salvation. Their actions showed their faith.

Are we prepared to do as he asks or do we settle for pious aspirations? How we actually live gives the answer.

Twenty-seventh Sunday in Ordinary Time

Mt 21:33-43

It has happened in many families. Through diligent hard work and perhaps a little luck, one generation put together a tidy farm, prosperous business or substantial savings. Then, with little appreciation of what has been handed on, the next generation neglects the inheritance and loses it completely. In today's gospel, Jesus is pointing out to the Jews of his own time that this is exactly what is happening to them. Through God's choice, through exile and suffering, through great leaders and teachers, the Jews had been fashioned into a people who knew the one true God and who were entrusted with the special role of bringing God's own Son into the world of their time. Theirs was a unique inheritance, a priceless vocation and they squandered it.

Could something similar be happening in our own lives and in our own land? There is no doubting the value of our inheritance. Tested through persecution and deprivation, faith in the one true God and in Jesus Christ born of Mary, has been entrusted to us. We are in danger of squandering our inheritance and leaving nothing but baubles for the next generation. Accumulating possessions, we have lost sight of the ingredients of lasting happiness. Fidelity, generosity, neighbourliness, forgiveness, heroism, and an awareness of God's love and presence were the hallmarks of what we received. They must be handed on or our inheritance will be given to another people. Today's warning of rejection is as applicable to us today as it was to the people of Jesus' own time.

Twenty-eighth Sunday in Ordinary Time

Mt 22:1-14

Advertising by commercial development agencies often features individuals who had a good idea and who also had the initiative and willingness to follow it up. Each of those featured is now running a successful small business. They recognised an opportunity for what it truly was and they made the most of it. In different ways, each of us is called to do something similar in our relationship with God. Failure in life is to miss recognising God in the circumstances of our daily lives. It is the inability or unwillingness to see the opportunity he offers to know him more clearly, to serve him more generously and to be secure in his love. The Jews of Christ's time were blind to that opportunity and so lost out. In an attempt to alert them to what they were missing out on, Christ used the image of a marriage feast to which many of the invited guests failed to turn up. They did not realise what they were missing. Outsiders saw their chance and came but even among them, some were not prepared to enter fully into the spirit of the celebrations. Maybe they only came for the drink. Anyway, they too were rejected. As well as recognising an opportunity, one must be prepared to pay the price of personal change in following it.

Today's gospel challenges us to recognise God in daily life and, recognising him, to be changed in heart and lifestyle. The temptation is to settle for mediocrity when we are given the opportunity of being truly great as children of God.

Twenty-ninth Sunday in Ordinary Time

Mt 22:15-21

Questions quite often make statements or set traps rather than merely seek information. The query, 'Do you expect me to believe that story?' is usually saying that the enquirer thinks you are either untruthful or naive. Sometimes the deviousness or the cowardice of the questioner is not immediately obvious to the uninitiated. As we read in today's gospel, Jesus was not fooled when the obsequious Pharisee asked his advice about paying taxes to Caesar. The Pharisee hoped to inveigle Jesus either into trouble with the Romans or into losing popularity with his own people. Seeing through the malice of the questioner, Jesus neatly side-stepped the question and used the occasion to teach that civil institutions have important legitimate authority. To be genuine, this authority must always be based on the truth. The fundamental truth is that each person is unique, with inalienable rights to life, to food, to shelter, to safety, to family, to living according to one's conscience, to freedom of expression and of religion.

There is a basic equality between persons no matter what their race, age or religion. It is the duty of civil authority to protect this equality and, when it fails to do so, it loses its real authority. In the plan of creation, one person should never be used or abused to satisfy the selfishness of another.

Each human person's destiny reaches beyond the limitations of the material world, but it is in and through this creation that God accomplishes his plan for each one of us. The splendour of this truth is the source of our hope. It is the role of the church to continually present this truth as the beacon of our life journey.

Thirtieth Sunday in Ordinary Time

Mt 22:34-40

Selfishness is strong and well in us and around us. Self-love is much less common. There is a difference between them. Selfishness makes oneself the centre of things. Its only concern is with one's own success, comfort and wellbeing. The main thrust is inwards. Selfishness looks outward only to get. Self-love looks outward to give. It first looks inward to recognise its own talents and gifts but sees them as opportunities to enrich the lives of others. This leads to an outward reach that is built on the solid foundation of accepting one's uniqueness and goodness at this time and in this place. It is a realisation that, made and loved by God as we are, we are precious in his eyes and in our own. If we are loved by God, we must surely love ourselves.

In today's gospel, Christ challenges us to love our neighbours as ourselves. Unless our self-love is genuine, giving the neighbours parity will not benefit them greatly. True self-love is nurtured through prayer of thankfulness to God. The hallmarks of selfishness are anxiety and fear. The fruits of self-love are gratitude and joy.

Thirty-first Sunday in Ordinary Time

Mt 23:1-12

One of the great impoverishments of our time is the lack of creative and life-giving authority. The tragedy is that authority, which is intended to be an enabling and supportive gift, is often experienced by many as a restrictive burden. This is true in different ways in the family, in school, in sport, in industry and in the church. The reasons for this situation in a rapidly evolving world are complex and indeed intimidating. The temptation is to bemoan the passing of the security which powerful authority gave to another era and to do nothing to enable powerless authority to enrich society today.

All authority is time-conditioned in how it is exercised and received. But at all times, it is the particular responsibility of those in leadership roles or positions of control to ensure that authority nurtures respect-filled relationships between all members of the community in their varied situations and with their particular gifts. Today's gospel has harsh words for those who fail to take that responsibility seriously.

It is the leader's task to evoke the trust that allows people to overcome their fears of being exploited or misled and so to accept the guiding hand of another fellow pilgrim on life's journey. It is only through heroic self-giving and wise service that such trust is nourished, a trust that nobody is entitled to undermine. Each of us is called to create and protect genuine authority by affirming the courage of the unselfish leader and by building up the wisdom authority needs. All true authority is God's gift to his people. Such a gift must be made present in every age through those who are called to be saints, you and I.

Thirty-second Sunday in Ordinary Time

Mt 25:1-13

As I write, two deer are nibbling a few yards away. With the arrival of colder weather, diminishing food supplies higher up the Killarney mountains have driven them to forage closer to human habitation. Hungry they may be but still they are ever alert to any sound or movement that might indicate a rival or an enemy. They could be models of responses to today's gospel, where Jesus uses the parable of the wise and foolish bridesmaids to warn us about the necessity of being always prepared for the coming of God in our lives.

The essence of human happiness is to be able to recognise and tune into the presence of God and his plan for us in every aspect of daily life. The temptation is to be so self-centred that we put off the encounter with God and live as if it will come in a more dramatic way sometime in the future, and certainly not now. But now is what we have. The invitation is to be alert to every opportunity of serving the neighbours, of forgiving the offender, of affirming the good, of praising the Lord and growing in his friendship. The warning is to sense and avoid anything that endangers faith, corrodes hope or undermines love.

The deer have spotted me and moved away. In their lives, there are more important things than the lush grass on the front garden. Freedom and safety are too precious to them to be risked for transient pleasure. Today is an opportunity to clarify what is closest to our hearts and what must be sacrificed to protect it. We all need the vigilance of the deer.

Thirty-third Sunday in Ordinary Time

Mt 25:14-30

Possessiveness is the cancer of our society. Rampant on every side and within us, it is an attitude of mind and heart that sees one's own security, wellbeing and comfort as the most important things in life. It uses power to extract the maximum personal benefit from every situation, no matter what the cost to others. It is a form of idolatry that behaves as if we were the creators of our own lives and of our own destiny. It is so pervasive in our culture that it touches each one of us to some degree whether we like it or not.

It is like dry rot that, unnoticed, destructively undermines our Christian lifestyle and our communities. It is seen where privilege protects the well off, where restrictive work practices limit opportunity, where minority groups are victimised, where religious resources are focused on the maintenance of the saints rather than on the evangelisation of the world, where politics substitutes cant for courage and tradition for vision, where fear drives any one of us to protect our own patch against another's needs.

In today's gospel of the talents, Jesus teaches strongly that all God's gifts, including personal talents, are given for the good of all his people. Such teaching turns current attitudes upside down.

Jesus asks each of us to examine where we stand on such basic issues. He will convert us to his way of living if we really want it, but maybe we do not want it.

Our Lord Jesus Christ, Universal King

(Thirty-fourth Sunday in Ordinary Time)

Mt 25:31-46

Joe's query was not out of concern for my welfare but rather to highlight his own predicament. He merely asked whether I had eaten a meal that day. He had not, and with the frosty evening closing in he was not likely to eat one unless I provided it. One way or the other, he assured me that he would survive, as there were many days when he did not have a decent meal but it would be greatly appreciated if he could have one now. Like an alert T.D., he quickly added the supplementary question to ask if I had ever gone two days in winter without a meal. The plea was irresistible.

When Joe left, I was filled with gratitude towards and deep appreciation of the thousands of people throughout the land who provide meals on wheels, who care for ageing or sick relatives or neighbours, who work in the Vincent de Paul Society, Simon or the aid agencies. Today's gospel is a salute to all such workers and helpers. Jesus assures them that every act of kindness done to one in need is done to himself and will be rewarded accordingly. It is an encouraging and challenging reassurance. For those of us who choose to ignore the opportunity to feed, clothe or house the needy brother or sister, the gospel warning is very ominous.

It is a good gospel to keep before our minds in the run up to Christmas.

St Patrick's Day

Lk 10:1-12, 17-20

Being Irish today is both a sought-after privilege and a vehemently rejected designation. A significant number of people born on this island do not regard themselves as Irish and do not wish to be so regarded. Yet, many emigrants' children born abroad certainly regard themselves as Irish and see such Irishness as their birth right. To be Irish is other than and more than place of origin or lineage, though both are strands in the tapestry. To be a sharer in the spiritual legacy of St Patrick is a more challenging privilege than being Irish. It is to share in a bonding influence that is at once both an inheritance and an ongoing creation. Some strands of the inheritance must be surrendered such as a sense of resentful anger against past oppressors. Other strands must be owned, nurtured and enriched. Faith in God as Father, Son and Holy Spirit is central. It is not without reason that folklore has attributed to Patrick the use of the three-leafed shamrock as an aid to his teaching on the Trinity. A treasure of Patrick's time almost lost to later generations but now gradually being rediscovered and appreciated, are the scriptures, God's written word. But God spoke first through his creation and for centuries Irish spirituality had a deep sense of God present in nature and in the ordinary events of human living. All God's creation is sacred. True followers of St Patrick must be in the vanguard of ecological concern to safeguard God's creation. The pinnacle of that creation is human life. Its protection is as fundamental to our heritage as it must be to the future ethos of our culture. Peace is our priority now. Lasting peace can only be built on absolute respect for all human life. In any culture, double standards about fundamentals leads to chaos and to the self -destruction of the culture. On the other hand, a caring concern for one another, that recognises and protects the uniqueness of each person and that straddles all social classes and religious differences, can surely build up a heritage of faith, peace and love that will be a credit to St Patrick and a beacon of hope in a despairing world.

The Assumption of the Blessed Virgin Mary

Lk 1:39-56

In Dublin in the seventies, at a peace concert in the RDS, the Freshmen won many new fans with a song called *When God Created Woman, He Created Love*. A line in the song said that he bestowed on her a new gift of love. This was certainly true when God created Mary and destined her to be the mother of his only Son. His choice made Mary special from the first moment of her conception until the moment when he took her home, body and soul, to himself for ever. This final gift to her is what we call the Assumption – the feast we remember today.

From the beginning Mary realised rapidly enough the awesomeness of her destiny. While she did wonder at the Annunciation how she could be a virginal mother, she entrusted herself to the Lord who had called her. Despite Joseph's doubts and neighbours' gossip, she grew into an ever-deepening joyful appreciation of the great things he was accomplishing in her and through her. This joy found expression in the Magnificat which is the core of today's gospel. God chooses the simple ordinary ones of this world to confound the proud of heart.

Mary's call was a very common one. It was to be a mother. Mary saw this as God's way of allowing her to have an unique part in the salvation of the world. He has a unique call for each of us and invites us, too, to make salvation present in our day. Ours is a glorious calling. We can join Mary in the Magnificat in praising our God for his goodness to each of us and his special gracing of Mary, our mother.

Mission Sunday

Mt 9:35-37

One of the great joys of my present job is to share in the varied vocation experiences of the students with whom I live. Apart from working in factories, building sites, services, maintenance, parishes, presbyteries and schools in Britain, France, Germany, Italy and the U.S.A. as well as in Ireland, some have been with our missionaries in Chile, Kenya, Pakistan and Bangladesh. So many of them met somebody I knew. Each one brought the same message. Every missionary friend wished to be remembered.

To be remembered is very important to everyone of us but it is especially important to those who have given their lives to bringing the good news of salvation to other peoples on our behalf.

It is on our behalf that they have gone out. The gift of faith brings with it the responsibility of sharing it. That is every Christian's responsibility and every parish's privileged duty. Our missionaries abroad undertake to fulfil that communal task in a special way. They are the frontline workers in what is everybody's business.

They are entitled to be remembered. Mission Sunday invites us to focus on our brothers and sisters, neighbours and friends, old school mates and acquaintances, all our fellow countrymen and women who have left home to preach Christ crucified and risen. The invitation is to remember them in prayer before the Lord today and everyday, to write the letter of remembrance, to dig deep into our pockets to finance their meagre living and their work.

Above all, the invitation of this Mission Sunday is to pray that others will follow to continue the task so well done by Irish missionary over the last hundred years. Surely, the real heartbreak for any missionary must be to see his or her life's work collapse due to lack of personnel or finance.

Missionaries for Christ, it is our privilege to remember you on Mission Sunday.

All Saints

Mt 5:1-12

Even though bachelor brothers, Joseph and John, seemed to be as different as chalk and cheese, they lived out retirement together contentedly in the family home. Joseph was deeply religious, attending Mass and spending long hours in prayer daily. It was years since John had attended church, chapel or meeting. Joseph's fervour seemed only to strengthen John's indifference. Quickly on the heels of Joseph's death, after a long illness bravely borne, John was snatched from life without warning as he went to vote. His drinking, gambling, non-practising confrères were shocked into silent anxious grief. But reassurance was quickly on the way. The father of the brotherhood was heard to proclaim, with the fervour of an experienced funeral preacher, that there was no need to worry as John would fly in on Joseph's surplus. It was an earthly and personalised exposition of the doctrine of communion of saints.

We believe that all the baptised, living and dead, form the people of God, the Body of Christ. If one part of the body is in need, the other parts protect it and carry it through to the fullness of life. Surely, Joseph's constant prayer for John must ensure that his brother is with him today as we celebrate the Feast of All Saints. This is the day we celebrate the safe arrival home to heaven of our departed brothers and sisters. It is festival day for those who deserve it (and they are few) and also, for all those for whom Jesus, our brother, prayed and died on Calvary. We all hope to fly in on his surplus and we surely will once we have declared our candidature on his ticket. That is today's reassurance, with its invitation to live like the brother full of gentleness, purity, forgiveness and detachment.

Today is an opportunity to talk to our brother about how we are doing and to remind him that he has told us that he was going to prepare a place for us and that, when he has it ready, he will take us safely home. Let us pray for each other that we will be ready to go when the final count is declared.

The Immaculate Conception

Lk 1:26-38

In stressing childhood experiences as central in the formation of one's character and personality, contemporary educationalists are emphasising what wise people always knew. A child who lives where giftedness outweighs limitation, where co-operation overrides competition, where respect for others as well as for oneself is tangible, where love is all-pervasive, such a child is being touched by God and is open to being responsive to the truly great plan God has for everyone of us. Such must have been the home experience of Mary, mother of Jesus. Certainly, God had prepared the mother of his Son from her conception, as we celebrate in today's feastday. But the seed of grace sown then had to be nurtured in a faith-filled family to enable her to be in tune with God's unique call to her at the annunciation.

The grace Mary received at conception, we receive at baptism. For most of us, home is where that gift must blossom first of all, not only in childhood but throughout our lives. To help another person to be tuned to God's individual call to them, is to equip them for life's most important purpose.

As we praise God today for Mary's Immaculate Conception, we thank him for the gift of our baptismal faith. Our own seed of faith may be dormant or blossoming. Either way, now is a good time to enrich it so that we may be on God's wavelength in every aspect of our lives. It would be tragic to be tuned to a third rate programme for life while God was inviting us on another channel to greatness and glory. Fine tuning the heart to God every day is the only way to a fulfilling life experience. Mary never settled for less. Neither should we.

Year B

First Sunday of Advent

Mk 13:33-37

Few people learn from experience. Many repeat the mistakes of previous generations as history shows. Our generation is no exception. On every side people go it alone, inattentive to the gracious presence of God and oblivious of the plight of the poor. In this state of unawareness, selfishness waxes strongly while hope decays rapidly into despair. God is more ignored than rejected. His people are crushed by the trials of life. The temptation is to desert him to seek security in possessions and to confuse happiness with pleasure.

Advent is God's rallying cry to his people before Christmas. Isaiah highlights how limited we are without the power of God and he compares us to clay in the hands of a potter. He pleads with God to rescue us from our inadvertence to him. The gospel cry of Jesus to be on our guard and to stay awake alerts us to the reality that self-interest always hinders our response to God. On the other hand, Paul is loud in his praise and thanks for the converts at Corinth who have responded so fully to God's gifts to them. Together there is a pressing invitation to be attentive during these weeks to the wonder of God among us. Let us make space and time for him in prayer during this Advent season. It will be well rewarded.

Second Sunday of Advent

Mk 1:1-8

The paradox of our relationship with God is that everything has been given to us and yet everything remains to be done. This is certainly the apparent contradiction of Advent. Jesus has come and yet we are challenged to prepare for his coming again.

It may seem confusing but there is something parallel in family life. Parents have given life to their child. This is the foundation of their relationship and still, as the years go by, this relationship between them is continually changing while yet remaining constant.

There is always room for surprises and indeed for disappointments in such a relationship; a constant core in varying contexts; gifts given and responded to; kindness shown and not reciprocated; encounters filled with joy and meetings devoid of love.

Through it all, the parent-child bond is an unchanging reality, sometimes ignored but often celebrated. The celebration revitalises the relationship and awakens a new appreciation of the unbreakable bond.

Christmas is the celebration of such an unbreakable bond. We are children of God. To celebrate such a privilege demands preparation. A basic preparation must be between the children themselves. Old scores must be forgiven, not settled. The impoverished ones must be fed, clothed and housed.

There must be a reaching out to those who feel they no longer belong. This reaching out must be done by individuals, families and by every parish. By linking with a brother or sister in need, each of us in her or his own way can prepare the way for the new coming of our first born brother, Jesus Christ, Our Lord.

Third Sunday of Advent

Jn 1:6-8, 19-28

Ours is fast becoming the age of the anonymous Christian. On every side there is pressure to restrict religion to being a very private individual matter. The attitude often is a condescending tolerance of one's right to follow Jesus provided that this does not impinge on the world at large. The temptation to restrict one's faith in this cosy cocoon is as insidious as it is pervasive. The suggestion is that one may be as charitable as one likes but one must not stand up for justice for the deprived. Fidelity is fine as long as it does not challenge the promiscuous. Public expressions of faith must be downplayed lest they offend the sensitivities of the sophisticated. Any comfortable lifestyle is acceptable as long as it cloaks the witness to which Jesus calls us. Today's gospel tells of one person who did not take refuge in anonymity but openly declared his allegiance when challenged by his contemporaries. John the Baptist paid with his life for his open loyalty to Jesus. He died as a witness to the truth he believed in. It is a frightening scenario. Yet, to live like Jesus and to bear witness to him in every aspect of our lives, will often only be done at great personal cost. The strengthening consolation is that such courage is well rewarded and he will enable us to bear witness to him if we trust him. It is the royal road to true happiness.

Fourth Sunday of Advent

Lk 1:26-38

Last week, I was at a very talented song contest. Throughout the night, the limelight moved back and forth from the compere to the backing groups and on to the guest artists. But of course, it focused again and again on the singers themselves. For on that night, it was they who were centre stage. Everybody realised that without them there would be nothing to celebrate.

Today's gospel reminds us that it was a woman who was centre stage at the first Christmas. It was a woman who brought Christmas to the world. It is still true that so often it is women who continue to bring Christ to men and men to Christ. Today is an opportunity to say thanks to the women who sowed the seeds of faith in our hearts, who nurtured God's love within us, who through their tenderness and love have brought many to know the mercy of God. Women do not need liberation. Instead, they are entitled to our appreciation, and our recognition of the glory of God's call to them. Without Mary's response to God, there would not have been a first Christmas. Without women's faith today ...

Let today be women's day in the run up to Christmas.

Christmas Day

Lk 2:1-14

The small children's school nativity play ended in total confusion. It had started so well with Joseph proudly setting out for Bethlehem assuring Mary that all would be well when they got to their own kingly town. After all was not he himself one of the royal family! In the crowded census town he played his part superbly as he pleaded for lodgings from the harassed innkeeper played by a neighbour's child. Then the play collapsed. As the budding shepherds waited to scamper to the cave and the ox and the ass grew evermore impatient, the innkeeper, overcome with compassion, invited the expectant mother in to share the crowded house. What now!

As she explained later, her own mother never turned anyone away from their door, so she could not do so to the mother of Jesus nor to the boy next door. Her heart proved to be bigger than her expected role and her world was totally disconcerted as a result. This is the essence of the Christmas message and experience. The almighty God who keeps all creation in the palm of his hand, steps beyond that role and out of love, sends his only Son to share our human life. He does it so that we will experience energising and reassuring love in the fibre of our beings. Stepping out beyond the expected, love was made real for the whole human race at the first Christmas.

So it can be at every Christmas. Each time any one of us surprises ourselves by extravagant generosity, uncharacteristic forgiveness or heroic service, we step out of our conventional role and create oases of love in our desert world. In doing so, we risk respectability, ridicule and rejection. Without risk, we cannot imitate a God who, in sharing his own divine life, kept nothing for himself exclusively. To live like him is to risk letting in the stranger, welcoming the poor, trusting in God for tomorrow, keeping nothing for oneself or one's family exclusively. It is a challenge that does not bear thinking about. It could be so frightening and so demanding. But the birth of Jesus reassures us that God is with us now and always. His presence within and among us enables us to step beyond our limited selves again and again and so bring true love to everyone whose lives we touch this Christmas.

May the peace of Christ reign in our hearts and in our homes at Christmas and always.

Holy Family

Lk 2:22, 39, 40

The pain of parting flickers alive once more as the great exodus begins again. More people than every returned home for Christmas. The booming overseas traffic figures show the central place of emigration in the fabric of our society. But these statistics also indicate the enduring strength of family bonds among our people. Our young and not so young emigrants want to celebrate family by their presence as well as by their presents. They glimpse that family is the source and the nutrient of what is most precious within themselves as persons. Some realise that they never appreciated family fully until they had left it. Something similar can happen to each of us. We often do not appreciate the best things in life until they are lost to us. We take health, employment, faith and friendship for granted until we no longer have them. Then bemoaning their loss is futile.

Today's Eucharist is a celebration of the treasure of family. It is a reminder that family, like all precious things, needs to be protected and fostered. Family is the first source of faith, hope and love, the centre where we are enabled to trust and be trusted, to forgive and be forgiven, to know God and to be known to him, where we experience unconditional belonging which mirrors the unconditional love of God. When family fulfils these roles, the dwelling place of God is built up among us. When selfishness or infidelity undermines family, the core of God's creation is undermined. Each day we build up or we undermine.

There is no middle way.

Second Sunday after Christmas

Jn 1:1-18, Eph 1:15-18

Joan has a tough life always. Her alcoholic husband has grown more irresponsible and wayward over the years. Despite this the family has done well and are successful in their well-paid careers. Distressed at seeing their mother's continuing hardship, they plead with her to live with one of them or else, in a new home of her own which they could provide. She refuses and stays with her husband. Many would not understand her heroism nowadays. Her explanation is simple yet profound. She loves her man. For Joan, love is freely given. It can never be earned or deserved. It is pure gift. Once she promised it forever and she is faithful to that promise every day. In her self-effacing generosity we see love made present in daily living. It is unconditional love made flesh. It was such love that inspired God to send his Son among us, born of the Virgin Mary. Today's gospel is a hymn of praise and joy about this Son, the word of God, taking flesh among us out of sheer love to shatter the darkness of selfishness and to show the reckless generosity of the Father.

Blessed be God, the Father of our Lord Jesus Christ, who has blessed us with all spiritual blessings in Christ. He chose us to live through love in his presence. He has called us to imitate his love in our daily living following the example of Jesus and Joan who both give their lives for those they love.

Epiphany

Mt 2:1-12

The first Christmas was an almost hidden event. God became human but nobody knew except Mary and Joseph and a few shepherds. Even they did not realise the full meaning of what had happened. Then the wise men came from the East to acknowledge that this infant was a special one sent by God. The coming of Magi was to show that God took on human nature not just for the chosen people but to save all people. The enterprising trio followed God's inspiration, found Christ and brought the good news back to their own people. They were not distracted from that task even by Herod's invitation to return and enjoy his royal hospitality.

As we move into the next century, people everywhere will need to hear and heed the fact that God has visited his people and lives in our world. On the feast of the Epiphany, we ask for an outpouring of the Holy Spirit upon us so that, like the Magi, we will follow God's call and, finding Jesus ourselves, we will not be distracted from bringing him to our own people and others during the coming year.

Baptism of the Lord

Mk 1:7-11

As Sonia O'Sullivan's fame grows, so does the significance of her first victory in a cross-country race. It is now seen as a key moment in her athletics career. Dated photographs acquire due recognition somewhat belatedly. Today's gospel is a memory word-picture of the first time Jesus caught the public eye and of course, it was written long after the miracles and Calvary had brought fame and notoriety.

The scene was not altogether unusual because Palestine at the time had many itinerant preachers who proclaimed their dire warnings where people gathered. Apart from his desert diet and hippie dress, what made John the Baptist different was that people sensed something special about him and went out of their way to hear him. So he set up near the Jordan where he immersed people in the river as a sign of their willingness to leave sin behind and to make a fresh start in how they lived.

As well as his unrelenting call to repentance, John was continually alerting people to the coming of God's chosen messenger. So he must have been delighted and taken aback when Jesus arrived to be immersed in the river Jordan. John felt unworthy but did as Jesus asked him. Even though John continued his preaching of repentance, this occasion marked the end of his work of preparation for the coming of his cousin, the Messiah. For Jesus, the occasion was the beginning of the public life which will be the source of our gospel stories throughout the year ahead. Mark is the reporter this year. Follow his byline.

Ash Wednesday

Mt 6:1-6, 16-18

As an inducement to buy, product advertising often promises a huge percentage discount over the listed price. Rather than vouching for the quality of the product, this approach shows that the original price was exorbitant and that earlier buyers did not get value for their money at all. But the intended message of such advertising is that only the foolish would now let this new offer pass. The aim is to lull the unwary into believing subconsciously that the advertiser's motivation is benevolence rather than profit. Advertising is rarely what it seems to be at first sight. There is usually a hidden agenda, something more than meets the eye.

This is true also in the presentation of Lent and, more especially, of Ash Wednesday. The cryptic one-liner that may accompany the ashes is 'remember that you are dust and to dust you will return'. It is a stern warning that death awaits each of us sooner rather than later. The most obvious message is that unless we give up our selfishness, we are doomed. But there is a somewhat hidden agenda. There is more to Lent than heroics and self-denial, important though these are. While it is not a commercial break in the whirlwind of daily living, Lent is a lived out reminder that the cross of Calvary is the advertisement of God's love for us. In this situation, the advertiser pays the price of our everlasting life and the cross vouches for the fact that one's life is worth so much to God that he died for each one of us. There are no percentage discounts. God's gift of love is total, unconditional and forever.

Lent is an ongoing advertisement of God's offer of himself. We are invited to absorb this love and to make it present daily in our world through justice, truth, generosity and forgiveness. Only the foolish or the unbeliever could pass up such an opportunity.

First Sunday of Lent

Mk 1:12-15

When I was a young boy, Anthony Eden was reputed to be every woman's fancy. According to many of the pub's customers, his handsome looks created many interesting and tempting situations for him. One small little man, Johnny, was sitting on a high stool listening pensively to stories of Eden's supposed prowess. Johnny himself was somewhat less than handsome. His comment was cryptic. 'Thank God, I was not born good looking.' His limited attractiveness relieved him of some temptations, he felt. However, I am sure that Johnny still had his own temptations as we all have. Even Christ was tempted as we hear in today's gospel. For him, the temptation was to selfishness and self-centredness, to accept security and fame for himself. His response was to reject these passing joys and opt for the Father's will which led to the cross before the glory of the resurrection.

This temptation to selfishness is the same for each of us. For some, it may have become so ingrained and habitual that we no longer even recognise our areas of self-centredness. Such blindness is a great affliction. It prevents us following the road to true happiness. Lent is an opportunity to ask God to open our eyes to our smugness and to fill our hearts with courageous generosity towards our brothers and sisters everywhere.

Second Sunday of Lent

Mk 9:2-10

To be special to somebody is a privilege that meets one of our deepest human needs. Being aware of this privilege nurtures deep-seated joy even in the midst of difficulties and suffering. However, this awareness is often blocked by fears, insecurities, resentment, anger, addictions and by the pressures of life. To be conscious of being loved, one must make space to allow the power of the loving one to touch and heal one.

As we read in today's gospel, Jesus made that space when he went up the mountain with Peter, James and John to be alone with the Father in their presence. There he heard the Father assure him, 'You are my beloved' and that assurance changed him so much that the trio were visibly shaken but knew it was good to be with him. The Father offers us a similar option. He wants each of us to know that we are special to him, truly beloved.

If we make ourselves open to receive the gift of a growing awareness of his constant love, it will fill us with a secure peace. This deepening peace will not make us shine like the sun but will create an atmosphere in which it will be tangible that God is with us. Being aware of this mystery is our privileged joy.

Third Sunday of Lent

Jn 2:13-25

Actions speak louder than words. This was as true in the time of Jesus as it is today. Jesus did not argue with the Sadducees and the Scribes about the traders and the money changers in the Temple. He acted and he acted dramatically. He drove them out. His action showed clearly his belief that the Temple was firstly the focus of God's presence among his people and the focus of Jewish worship rather than a venue for turning a quick shekel no matter how honest or convenient. His teaching went on to point out that from then on his risen body, his permanent presence among us, is to be the focus of our worship. Zeal for this body must eat us up as zeal for the Jewish Temple devoured Christ. His teaching evoked a response because it had been accompanied by courageous and radical action. Mother Teresa's talks on love and life are heeded for the same reason. In our world, the gospel message often fails to evoke a response among the young and indeed the not so young. It is not that the gospel has lost its power but rather that believers, like you and me, fail to live the authentic lifestyle that Jesus invites us to live. 'Love one another as I have loved you' was his message. It must be the same for us. Our unconditional forgiveness, our unwavering fidelity, our unselfish friendship, our transparent truthfulness and our generous justice must always underpin our worship and our prayer. Only Jesus can enable us to undertake such a noble way of life and he will do so this Lent, if that is our deep desire.

Fourth Sunday of Lent

Jn 3:14-21

When Boney M soared to the top of the charts with *By The Rivers Of Babylon* few people stopped to wonder about the origins of the words.

As young people all over the world hummed the tune, few realised that this updated version of a great lament was the anthem hymn of the Hebrews during their exile. Today, it is the psalm linking the Old Testament reading with the gospel.

The reading tells how God allowed the chosen people to be punished by exile for their wrongdoings, but it ends with a note of hope that returning home is on the horizon.

God never forsakes the ones he has chosen. The gospel takes that message of faithfulness further. Not only does God welcome us home from the exile of sin to his friendship but he has sent his Son to ensure that we are able for the journey and arrive safely. The Son has come not to condemn our faults. Such condemnation would only crush us further. But he comes so that we will have eternal life, the spirit of courage, faith, generosity, the Spirit of God to strengthen us for the road home to his love.

The only question is whether we will believe this message in the depths of our hearts and live accordingly or not. The believer knows that God never deserts anyone.

Fifth Sunday of Lent

Jn 12:20-33

As spring slips by, it is fascinating to watch where daffodils grow. Often it is in some unlikely corner which a few weeks ago looked barren and neglected. Yet in that spot, despite appearances, the daffodil bulbs lay hidden but alive in the damp cold soil covered, perhaps, by last autumn's still decaying leaves. In such an unwelcoming seed bed, the bulbs germinated, sent out new shoots and grew into something beautiful for us and for God. If they were kept safely clean, warm and dry on a shelf they would eventually shrivel up and die without trace. Instead because they were entrusted to such an apparently hostile environment, they had the opportunity to bloom, multiply and enrich their surroundings. Such is the process of all seed sowing and harvesting.

It is this imagery that Jesus uses in today's gospel to teach us that he had to suffer the horror of Calvary to bring new life to the world. It is so difficult to grasp and appreciate why the gracious Christ endured such suffering and death. But he tells us that without a hidden germinating period, a period perhaps of pain and disappointment, there can never be an abundant harvest of goodness.

So too it is in our lives. We must continue to sow seeds of goodness and generosity even where they seem to be unwanted and ignored, yet believing that one day they will bear fruit a hundredfold. Sometimes we lose heart and we lose hope. The struggle can seem so pointless as Calvary must have seemed to be such a failure. But there was a resurrection after Calvary. So, too, for us there will be peace and joy even in suffering and death through the presence of Jesus who draws us to himself. Such is our faith.

Today is a day to renew that faith together and to keep hope alive in each other's hearts and lives. Never lose hope. With Jesus, a new spring always follows even the severest winter.

Passion Sunday

Mk 14:1-15, 47

Processions of all shapes, sizes and motivations are part of our human culture. No protest is complete without a procession. Almost every celebration demands one, however brief. Some processions are planned, even manipulated. Others arise spontaneously from people's need to express themselves. Some processions turn to tragedy. Others end in glory. Some processions are over as soon as they finish. Others have effects that last long into history. Processions may be simple and casual but even these can be very significant, telling what is in the heart of a people.

Jesus did not rent a crowd for his arrival in Jerusalem on Palm Sunday. He knew the feeling of the people and realised what a tumultuous welcome he would get. He also realised the consequences. So did some cute onlookers. There are always the cagey ones looking on at the procession which is life, who see the likely outcomes in favour of the powerful but will never risk their own comfort or good name to change things for the better, to right an injustice, to protect the defenceless, to challenge the established, to build peace.

On Palm Sunday, shrewd observers realised that the people in power could not just let Jesus rally the people any more. He would have to be taken care of. It would be better for themselves to lie low for the week until all would be over. Have things changed? Have we changed? Will we let this week change us? It could.

Good Friday

Jn 18:1-19, 42

The excitement of birth is twinned with the finality of death. At birth, the questioning is joyful and curious. What will this child be? There is a ripple of hope-filled anticipation. Life will continue. We will live on in our children. There is a new beginning. At death, the questioning can be sorrowing, sombre and heartrending.

Why death now? Why death ever? What is in store for our loved one now? What of the bereaved? The joyful anticipation is replaced with pain-filled loss and anxiety. Even in the presence of vibrant faith, there is often a sense of finality, of completion of an era.

This atmosphere of finality pervaded Calvary on Good Friday. The great hopes of a promising life were dashed. His closest friend, John, was shattered as he undertook to care for the mother who was desolate at the death of her one and only in his early thirties. What grief! What disappointment! With more care and sense, it could have been avoided.

With hindsight, it was easy to see that it would end in this way if he insisted on justice, forgiveness, love and peace. Now the miracle worker from Nazareth failed to come down from the Cross even though he had raised Lazarus from the dead. Dead he was now himself, the same as those who had gone before him.

But, not quite the same. Even though he died willingly in obedience to the Father's will, he had the power to take up his life again. That he would do at the Resurrection, but first he would endure the intense pain of the human condition. He must know the loneliness of death at first hand, the sense of abandonment by God.

Jesus truly walked the road of life before us, the full road to the end. He invites us today to be with him on his journey so that he may be more fully with us on our life journey, awakening our hearts to the hope of a new enriched life when death snatches this brief life from our grasp. This death is the gateway to eternal life. This is our faith.

'I believe, Lord. Help the little faith I have.'

Holy Saturday

Mk 16:1-8

Candles have long since been surpassed as a source of light except in emergency situations. But in romance, ritual and religion the candle retains a powerful symbolic meaning. For a recent television programme, the magnificent college chapel at Maynooth was lit with a battery of powerful lights that illuminated its treasures as never before and in a way that could not have been imagined a century ago when the chapel was built.

Tonight, the same chapel will be lit by a single candle. The magnificence will be hidden but the candle will be the symbol of treasures that can only be glimpsed at through faith, sought after in hope and accepted with love.

Here and in all our churches, the paschal candle will represent the risen Christ who by his passion, death and resurrection, has enabled us to share in and enjoy the love and life of God himself.

It is really a staggering privilege. To believe in it is a gift freely given, open to all who are willing to place their trust in Christ. The weekend is an opportunity to accept a gift of deepening faith that blossoms into hope-filled love. It would be a great loss to let it slip by unnoticed.

Easter Sunday

Jn 20:1-9

Hopelessness pollutes our life space. So many streams flow into the sea of our despair. Long term unemployment scars many a heart. Violence awakens fear in the vulnerable, young and old. Famine gnaws away the fabric of our society. Scandals in high places erode trust. Infidelity undermines family security. It gets easier and easier to paint a grim picture of pointless life ending in disastrous death. The darker the night, the more significant is the torch.

Our torch is the risen Christ. This Easter, as perhaps never before, Christ's message is vital for the people of our time. It is vital because it is life-giving. It is a message of hope highlighting that the God, who made the world and its people, has both safely in his hands and his helping is nearer than the air we breathe. In fact, he is living in our hearts and in our relationships. He has taken on our human condition even unto death. Rising from the dead, he has changed utterly the meaning of our lives.

We are made to love and to be loved, to reach out in forgiveness, generosity and trust to every brother and sister, especially those in greatest need. Following the torch of his example, we are called to keep hope alive for all those whose lives we touch, hope in the power of God's love working in and through us for one another. To undermine this hope is the essence of evil. Keeping this hope alive is the privileged calling and daunting challenge facing us as an Easter people.

Second Sunday of Easter

Jn 20:19-31

The doubting Thomas saga is often glibly used to dismiss even the most reasonable reservations about a project. Of course, it is frequently invoked by people who have long forgotten its gospel origin. Thomas is in the not uncommon situation of being remembered for his limitations rather than for his finer qualities. He was the courageous one who suggested that all the disciples should go and die with the Lord in Jerusalem when danger threatened the Master. He was honest and open in saying that he did not understand a word when Jesus was talking about being the way to the Father. But it is for his unwillingness to believe in the resurrection of Jesus that he has gone down in history. Yet, his hesitancy was understandable. The others believed because they had been in the presence of the Risen Lord. Without this personal experience they would not have been convinced.

Such direct experience is not given to us either. Instead, the seed of faith is offered. We are free to accept it or to reject it. The ethos of our lives will determine whether the seed will germinate in our hearts. Even when it finds a home in us, faith remains a seedling, needing nurturance through prayer and communal celebration. While still a seedling, it propagates quickly, awakening and strengthening faith in those with whom we share life. Despite his doubting, once he dramatically accepted the fact that Jesus was risen, Thomas committed his whole life to believing in the Lord and to sharing this treasure with the world. Our times need many Thomases. The next generation will not be found wanting if the young are challenged, encouraged and supported by living models of today's faith in today's world. To be such an inspiration to one another is a personal and community responsibility. We must not lose heart.

Third Sunday of Easter

Lk 24:35-48

The Easter cold spell caught us unawares. We had not expected fluttering snowflakes. We scurried back for discarded scarves and caps. Readjusting controls on central heating systems allevi- ated even the trivial discomfort for many but not for the poor and hungry. For some of them, it was the last straw after a long wet winter. So while we may be experiencing compassion fat- igue after a good deal of giving, many others are suffering en- durance fatigue after months of struggle to keep warm and fed.

In today's gospel, Jesus offers his disciples an opportunity to prove for themselves that he is truly risen, by giving him food to eat. 'Have you anything here to eat?' he says. The famine stricken of the world and, in particular, the poor of our own neighbour- hood ask us a similar question. It is our opportunity to prove that we really believe that Jesus is risen and that people in need are truly our brothers and sisters.

Even in the presence of the risen Christ, the disciples were hesi- tant to believe that the resurrection had happened. To reassure them, Jesus invited them to touch him and then they could be sure. We touch him in and through one another. What we do to one another, we do to him whether it is crucifixion or building up.

Are we as hesitant as the first disciples or does our caring touch- ing of the lives of the deprived confirm our faith that one day we will all rise again and live forever as the one family of God? Generous sharing enriches faith. Persevering service is the fruit of faith.

Fourth Sunday of Easter

Jn 10:11-18

To watch a young child take its first faltering steps across a room towards a mother's outstretched arms is a moment of intense joy and hope. The joy springs from the child's willingness to risk exploring a new way of living as it responds to the enabling invitation of one who has given it life. The hope is that the child's potential will develop to the full, making its unique contribution to the world of the future.

When a young person today responds to a call to priesthood or religious life, he or she is doing something quite similar and yet something quite different. The call comes from God, the giver of all life, talents and opportunities. It is a call to intimate friendship with the Lord so that one may spend one's whole life in full-time service of his people.

The risk in exploring the call is that one may find the call is not for one, or that the price is more than one is prepared to pay. As in successful marriage, the price of generosity is high but the rewards are great.

Risk-taking is essential for greatness. As the child must risk falling, if it is to move from crawling to walking, one must risk sacrifice and pain if one is to experience the joy of love and service. In life one cannot have security and growth.

Today's gospel story of the good shepherd laying down his life for his flock is an opportunity to reflect on how urgently the world needs Spirit-filled volunteers to make God's presence tangible in every sphere of living. The hope is that this generation will realise its potential to build God's kingdom on earth in its own unique way.

Fifth Sunday of Easter

Jn 15:1-8

Out walking yesterday morning I noticed that somebody has been very busy collecting the many branches blown off the trees recently. The thrifty provider has gathered the dead timber into piles to bring it home for the fire. The live branches on the trees also attracted my attention as they shoot new buds that will, in time, bear fruit again. It is the usual cycle of growth and decay and growth again. This is the simple image Jesus uses in today's gospel. If we break off from him, we die spiritually and are fit only for the fire like the dead timber. On the other hand as long as we remain linked with him, his love flowing through us like sap will ensure that we eventually will bear the fruit of good deeds. We may be only at the budding stage, but if we stay linked the harvest is certain because it is he who is supplying the power, not ourselves.

Unlike the vine of Christ's time and place, the trees around here are lime, elm, beech and chestnut but the message is the same, namely, broken off branches die. If we break off from Christ through sin, we will cease to bear the fruit of service that God intended us to produce. The invitation is to stay linked with Christ present in his church.

Sixth Sunday of Easter

Jn 15:9-17

At the time of writing the gospels, the Greek language had two words for love. *Eros* meant romantic love. The wise Greeks knew that there was much more to real love than infatuation and physical pleasure and they used another word, *agape*, to describe the love that is rooted in self-giving, that blossoms in adversity, that develops into community leading to lasting joyful fidelity and peacefilled security.

It is this word *agape* that was used in Sunday's readings to describe, however inadequately, the love between the Father and Jesus. It is with this same love that God loves us and empowers us to love one another.

The core of this love is in the lover always taking the initiative, reaching out in goodness to the loved one. Such love can never be earned. It is always a gift freely given, hopefully evoking a loving response but never withdrawn, no matter what the response.

Such is the love which the Father has for us, as shown to us in Jesus, sent to be the sacrifice which takes away our sins. Sacrifice and forgiveness are the life-blood of love, divine and human. Without them tenderness dissolves into disillusion, joy into jealousy, trust into betrayal, respect into revenge. Through them and through the Holy Spirit, attraction is refined into commitment leading to patient kindness, always ready to excuse, to trust, to hope and to endure whatever comes. It is for this we are created and redeemed.

The Ascension of the Lord

Mk 16:15-20

Parting messages have their own impact. Many an emigrant vividly remembers the final admonition and blessing of a heart-broken parent. Often school leavers hold on for years to the parting wisdom of an inspirational teacher. Marriage break-up can leave a lifelong painful memory of hurtful things said. An employer can frequently recall the parting outburst of the sacked employee. Final words have the power to make or to break, to challenge or to crush, to inspire or to inhibit, to energise or to deflate.

Christ's words as he left his disciples on Ascension Day are no exception. His command was clear-cut. 'Go out to the whole world and proclaim the good news to all creation.'

Important though our own individual salvation is, the focus at Christ's parting is on the worldwide proclamation of the gospel. Of course, it is through living the gospel values that we best bring Christ's message to others but the wider missionary task is ever present.

Ascension Day is a reminder of what we are called to do. It is a duty in which we all share and must not shirk.

Seventh Sunday of Easter

Jn 17:11-19

The outlook was bleak. They had hoped for great things. But the man in whom they placed their trust was now leaving them. Christ was leaving the disciples. With his departure went all their life dreams. They were going to need God's protection as never before.

Christ prayed for them in their hour of need. He prayed that united in love, they would stick together, support each other in the trials and remain faithful to the one true God. His followers had been given to him by the Father and he was preparing to die to make sure of their loyalty. His prayer was not merely words but included the greatest sacrifice of all, his life.

Today's gospel is part of his prayer for his friends in danger. He makes the same prayer for us in our time. With Christ praying for us, how could we ever lose hope, no matter what the cross, no matter what the danger?

Today is a reassurance of his care for us. Each of us needs it often.

Pentecost Sunday

Jn 15:26, 27; 16:12-15

At home and abroad tragic violence evokes a deep sense of powerlessness in the face of evil. The anguished cry in many a heart and in many a community is to even glimpse a way forward out of hopelessness. As traditions and institutions that protected, however falteringly, values, relationships and communities in the past, rapidly disintegrate, one temptation is to seek security in self-righteousness or authoritarianism. Another temptation is to yearn for times past and out of fear to bolt the door against the reality of the world outside. The latter course of action was the one adopted by the shocked disciples when the senseless barbarity of Calvary deprived them of their leader, their friend and their hope. Even the brief appearances of the Risen Lord among them did not restore their confidence or their peace. But the miracle of Pentecost did do so. Jesus had promised them an Advocate, a helper, his own Spirit to live among them, and that promise was now fulfilled. The promised Spirit of truth transformed them. It empowered them to be witnesses to Jesus throughout the world beginning from Jerusalem, their home base.

This Pentecost weekend, the same Spirit of Jesus is promised and offered to us as believers. Our need is no less than that of the early disciples. The hope of the future is to allow ourselves to be inspired by the Spirit of Jesus guiding our actions, challenging our desires, empowering our service, evoking our forgiveness, informing our decisions and encouraging our goodness towards each other and towards the whole world.

Pentecost is a time to invoke that Spirit and to be responsive to its living within us.

Trinity Sunday

Mt 28:16-20

'The Taking of Christ' by Caravaggio continues to haunt me. A postcard reproduction of the face of Christ, taken from the painting, looks out at me across the room. It communicates pain, distress, disappointment, agony, patience but, above all, love. It evokes a response of gratitude, empathy, solidarity, communion and love in return for such great love. Its power is stupendous. Its value is immeasurable.

However, in a culture that insists on evaluating everything from sporting prowess to feminine beauty in terms of the money it can command, this painting has acquired a £20 million tag.

But price is an unreliable guide to reality and oftentimes it deflects us from appreciating the true value of what life has to offer. In fact, the most precious things in life can neither be measured, earned, owned, proven or priced. They are pure gift and the greatest gift of all is the gift of faith in God, Father, Son and Holy Spirit.

The Trinity is our human way of talking about the wonder that is God, revealed to us in Jesus and living in us through the Spirit. Living in that Spirit, we bask in the love God pours into our hearts, which enables us to love one another in the image of the Holy Trinity, in whose name we are baptised. Such is our heritage.

Trinity Sunday is a good day to reclaim our inheritance.

The Body and Blood of Christ

Mk 14:12-16, 22-26

The popularity of June weddings has generated a plethora of anniversaries throughout the month, with jubilees having pride of place. The usual centrepiece of such celebration is a meal for family and friends, who hopefully are bound together by cherished memories, shared values and social ties. Such anniversaries can be reminders and celebrations of enduring love, and also a pledge of ongoing fidelity. While each celebration is unique, tradition dictates certain rituals of cake, toasts and speeches to mark the key events on the journey through life.

A key event in the life of the Jews was their escape from Egypt and the anniversary for this milestone became the most significant festival in their religious calendar. It was steeped in traditional ritual requiring detailed preparations. So when Jesus sent the disciples to prepare for their Passover feast, it caused no surprise. But when he changed the traditional blessing over the bread and wine in order to give us his Body and Blood, the disciples must have been truly astounded and did not grasp the wonder of what he had done until the fullness of the Spirit came upon them.

The feast of Corpus Christi is a reminder and a celebration of God's gift of himself to us and a pledge of eternal life and resurrection. This is our faith and our hope.

Second Sunday in Ordinary Time

Jn 1:35-42

We live in a world of ever more distractions, where loneliness grows deeper and more widespread. The increasing number of television channels, of omnipresent discmans and more compact radios, ensures that we need never endure silence. Distraction is always available at the press of a button. Loneliness can be temporarily suppressed through the short drink or the quick fix. But distractions or drugs do not meet the longings of the human heart.

Our core longing is for intimacy, a sharing of heart, of commitment and love. Some confuse intimacy with pleasure and end up devastated and frustrated. Others ignore this longing through constant activity in business, sport and entertainment.

But like a seed buried under tarmacadam, the longing eventually surfaces clamouring for attention. At the end of the day, we are made for relationships, relationship with God and with one another. We are not created to be individuals just beavering away, even at the most worthwhile tasks, without reference to each other.

To be able to relate is a tremendous gift that must be appreciated and developed throughout life. To be willing to relate calls for decisions to reach out daily to neighbours and to God.

Relationship always involves an invitation and a response and it always changes us. In today's gospel, Jesus invites Andrew and a companion to come and see where he lived. They stayed until evening. The next day Andrew brought along his brother, Simon, who was deeply influenced on his first meeting with the Master.

God constantly invites us to come to him and to see what intimacy his friendship holds for us. Often, we distract ourselves so much that perhaps we hear only the demands of his love and we miss the treasure it offers.

Something similar can happen in our human relationships. We feel the risks in reaching out to others and this fear prevents us glimpsing the joy of sharing in the lives of others as God intended. Individualism undermines the creator's plan for human happiness. It is rampant in many of our hearts.

Today, the Lord Jesus invites us to come and see a better way to live.

Third Sunday in Ordinary Time

Mk 1:14-20

Promises are a cornerstone in human living. Promises made, promises fulfilled or broken, determine the course and quality of each person's life, of every nation's story and of the human race's destiny. The sincerity of our promises is the canvas on which our life tapestry is woven. A sturdy canvas will survive the wear and tear of life. A flimsy one is torn by the merest stress. Everybody can remember some promise freely given and duly honoured which continues to sustain life each day. The appreciative recalling of these promises enriches faith, inspires hope and generates love. The promises we have made and kept are a living image of God himself because our God has always been making promises and keeping them.

In today's gospel, we find Jesus promising to make four small-time fishermen into fishers of men if they are willing to follow him. There was a price to be paid, something to be left aside, a security to be abandoned if there were to be room for God in their restricted lives. They chose to trust his promise. We have the same option. The invitation is to leave behind selfishness and sin, comfort and cynicism, revenge and regret. In return, he promises to make us into a people of prayer, sharers in his life, carers of each other, builders of peace, believers in the good news that Jesus loves each one of us personally and unconditionally.

Will we trust his promise? Can we afford not to?

Fourth Sunday in Ordinary Time

Mk 1:21-28

Ours is the age of opinions. Each of us feels entitled to have an opinion about everything. Opinion is dislodging truth as the acceptable guideline for living. The search for truth is often replaced by collecting the opinions of the articulate who may be no better informed than ourselves. Some opinions are based on truth, others on falsehood, more on ignorance and many on a mixture of all three. So, all opinions, especially many of our own, must always be suspect.

Truth is not always easy to ascertain by searching, for it is at the core of being human. Taking the lazy way out and settling for mere opinion about the significant aspects of life's journey shortchanges our human dignity. Truth about life is a treasure beyond compare. Finding it again and again is the peak of human achievement. Jesus came to enable us to do just that and to guide us on route. In today's gospel, we find his hearers riveted by the authority of his teaching. They sensed that here was a person who knew the truth unmistakably and who was prepared to lead them to it.

The power of his miracles attracted their attention but it was the commitment to the Father in his teaching that transformed their hearts. His authority sprang from utter conviction about the love of the Father for us. Today, he teaches us the same truth with the same love-filled authority, if only we have the wisdom to listen with joy in our hearts.

Fifth Sunday in Ordinary Time

Mk 1:29-39

'It is who you know that matters' is the firm belief of so many people. The disillusioned unemployed long for a contact to link them up with a job. Meanwhile, their self-esteem disintegrates as they sense from sad experience that reciprocal favours are more powerful than integrity and that contacts are more important than talent or need. There is a widespread conviction that ours is an insider's society. The accuracy of the perception may be questioned but the pervasiveness of the belief is unquestionable.

For some that belief will only be confirmed by today's gospel, where Jesus cures Peter's mother-in-law. They question why she received special treatment when there were many other sick people around pleading for a cure. Put that way, there is no clear-cut answer, but two indicative responses may help. Firstly, God knows best what we need most. Our greatest need may not be the one most obvious even to ourselves. Secondly, everything God gives is pure gift – life, health, love and talent. As we grow into a deeper appreciation of that giftedness of all God's blessings, we will grow into an awareness that all persons are equally precious in God's eyes, that each has a right to share in the earth's resources, that it is wrong to hoard in a shivering and starving world, that our concern must break through the insider ring to create a more just society for all. Painful though this will be, it is the road to lasting peace in the world. Everyone can start on it now.

Sixth Sunday in Ordinary Time

Mk 1:40-45

Many people vividly recall a particular event in their lives years after many similar events have been forgotten. Sportsmen may remember the match where they got their first score despite many better scores since. Some recall the details of their first wage packet even though later ones were more substantial. Other may recall the rain on the night they met their life partner despite all the torrents that have come since. In each case, the remembered event had a special significance for those involved.

This selective recall operated in the early church when the stories about the life of Jesus came to be written down. He had worked many miracles. Some were remembered more clearly than others. In today's gospel, Mark recounts the curing of the leper very early in the ministry of Jesus. For the Jews, leprosy was not only an incurable disease but it was erroneously seen as a sign of God's displeasure and punishment. Lepers were ostracised and forced to live apart from the socially acceptable community. Jesus broke through the conventions, touched the leper and cured him. Desperate for a cure, the victim had turned to Jesus as a last resort and his faith-filled hope was rewarded.

Sometimes in our desperation, we need to imitate the leper and challenge Jesus to cure us from sin, sickness, selfishness and self pity. Sometimes too, we need to step out beyond the conventions to minister to one another in our needs.

Seventh Sunday in Ordinary Time

Mk 2:1-12

The appearance of new shops specialising in health foods shows a constantly growing interest in such foods. A generation or two ago, most people would have hoped that all food was good for the health. On many sides, there are warnings about damaging one's health. Smoking is a particular target for the concerned. The attitude to butter is ambivalent. The powerful alcohol lobby ensures that no effective voice highlights its inherent dangers. Legions of devoted fans give extraordinary loyalty and discipline to promoters of particular products and lifestyles that promise beauty and physical well being. Few promoters of spiritual well being evoke a similar response apart from those who seem to offer physical healing as well. The instinct to seek physical well being is very dominant in all of us whereas it can be hard to advert to our need for spiritual healing and renewal.

Jesus faced a similar difficulty in his time. People were attracted by his miracles and flocked to be healed. As we read in today's gospel, men went so far as to take the roof off a house to get their paralysed friend into his presence. Their efforts were rewarded. But as soon as Jesus went on to teach that his miracles were meant to lead to faith in him as Son of God, he ran into opposition immediately. Something similar happens in our lives. In times of illness, we plead with God. When he offers spiritual healing in reconciliation, in persevering prayer, in the Eucharist, we are less than enthusiastic. The instinct to make care of the soul a priority is a weak one. It needs to be supported by disciplined commitment, shared faith and joyful celebration in love. Otherwise, we remain spiritual paralytics.

Eighth Sunday in Ordinary Time

Mk 2:18-22

Storytelling can communicate the most powerful message. The young and the not so young are often enthralled by the talented weaver of a good tale. Stories with powerful images can carry a message forward from one generation to the next. Jesus was aware of this power and used it very effectively as is shown in the stories of the good Samaritan and the prodigal son. He was also conscious of the potential of a good image like the vine and the branches and the good shepherd. However, if an image is to be really effective, the listeners must have direct personal experience of the reality underlying the image. The contemporaries of Jesus would have seen old wine skins recycled to hold new wine with disastrous results, as we read in today's gospel.

The impact of this image may be lost on those who use bottles rather than skins for storing their wines. But the challenge of the message has lost none of its topicality. Jesus was clarifying his position for any one who was thinking of being one of his followers. It would demand a whole new life style. It was not a matter of stitching on to one's jacket a badge saying 'I love Jesus'. Nor indeed, would weekly Sunday worship on its own be enough. To receive the treasures of new life he was offering would demand fundamental changes in attitudes in one's heart. It would demand commitment to him rather than conforming to religious rules.

The need for commitment to the person of Jesus was never greater. There is no place in his church for dormant, card-carrying members. The need is for apostolic witnesses who by the love of their lifestyle inspire others to seek this new wine of living in the presence of God as members of his family in every aspect of life in today's world. It is a daunting commitment.

Ninth Sunday in Ordinary Time

Mk 2:23-3:6

The controversy about Sunday trading rages on spasmodically. In some spheres the battle has been won or lost depending upon which side of the debate you support. The arguments range over individual freedom, customer choice, economic survival, premium payments, tourist needs, family values and religious traditions. The core purpose of keeping Sunday differently is being lost sight of in the confusion and inconsistencies of the arguments. A feature of the modern Sunday is its solitariness for many, and the exclusion of the deprived and the weak from many of its social activities. Individualism is coming to dominate our life style whereas we are created for relationship and community. To ignore the basic thrust of one's being is as foolish as it is prevalent.

The communal weekly rest day evolved to protect, nurture and develop the relationship aspect of human living. Not only was it a day for family time together but it was an opportunity for a neighbourhood to meet, to play, to care for each other and to celebrate together. At the heart of such celebrations was religious worship when the community acknowledged its indebtedness to the creator and expressed its joy in his goodness. As well as protecting its worship aspect, the churches, and sometimes the civil power, realised the enrichment potential of Sunday in human living and sought to protect it through suitable laws. But legislation on its own never adequately protects or nurtures the truly precious. The only thing that can make Sunday truly special is a renewed commitment to our interdependence as human persons and a deepening awareness of our dependence on the creator. When the thrust of human living is inordinately directed towards individual freedom, comfort and security at the expense of our potential and needs as a community, our world is out of balance. It is up to all followers of Jesus to restore the balance, no matter what the cost.

Tenth Sunday in Ordinary Time

Mk 3:20-35

Family is where one has roots and unbreakable bonds. These bonds may be supportive or suffocating, consoling or cruel, precious or painful but they remain always crucially influential. As they grow or decay, family relationships are lived out in varied ways but, no matter what happens, the link that comes from giving and receiving life remains rooted in the very core of our being. Nothing can break it and few things can surpass it in importance. However, in today's gospel, Jesus does give another bond, another relationship, greater priority. It is the relationship between a person and God, between the disciple and the Master.

The context was commonplace enough. As his preaching got more powerful and drew bigger and bigger crowds, family connections of Jesus were anxious about his emotional and mental stability. Out of deep concern for one of their own and, perhaps, prompted by his mother Mary, who went with them, they set out to bring him home where he could be looked after.

However, when Jesus was told of her presence, he used the occasion to teach forcefully that the strongest link anyone could have with him was to do the will of God. This teaching shocked the Jews because for them blood ties were supremely important, especially through the maternal line. But Jesus did not hold back and pointed out that Mary's greatness does not lie in being his biological mother, but rather in that she did the Father's will, unconditionally. This teaching is challenging and consoling because it shows that the way to true greatness and full discipleship with Jesus is open to each one of us every day.

Eleventh Sunday in Ordinary Time

Mk 4:26-34

On the window sills in many kitchens you will find young plants bursting into life. The phenomenon is repeated in schoolrooms all over the country, especially in primary schools. The young watch in awe as the small seed they have planted germinates, takes root and grows into blossom.

Children are often impatient and questioning during the germination which seems so long with little to show. Even growth does not always satisfy them as they long for flower or fruit.

In matters of faith, adults can be as impatient as children. The seed of God's kingdom sown in baptism, nurtured through prayer and Eucharist, can seem to be very slow in bearing fruit in service, gentleness and joyful peace.

But Christ assures us of the potential of this seed. He compares the faith-seed in our hearts with the tiny mustard seed which has the potential to grow into a tree. God's seed within us will always bear fruit unless it is stifled by fear or by preoccupation with oneself. God's call is not only to nurture one's own faith but to sow seeds of goodness wherever we are.

Never doubt the quality of his seed, and the soil of our hearts is his creation, too. Be of good heart and never tire of doing good.

Twelfth Sunday in Ordinary Time

Mk 4:35-41

Miracle workers usually evoke a lively reaction. People either dismiss them completely or else totally accept them and all that they stand for. The miracle worker is seen to have access to power beyond normal human capabilities and to be able to produce the extraordinary on demand. In that scenario, the miracle worker is given acclaim, deference and reward. Jesus had trouble in escaping that fate when he was instrumental in calming the storm, in healing the sick, and even in raising the dead to life. But in all such situations, Jesus went to great lengths to point out that the power came not from himself alone but from the Father who had sent him and that the purpose of the miracle was not to win admiration but to help the neighbour and to nurture faith in God.

In today's gospel, the storm-frightened disciples expected Jesus to care for them because it was to enable him to escape the crowds that they had set out to cross the lake in the first place. In their eyes, he owed them a favour. For varied reasons, we sometimes feel we should be spared some of the troubles of life. But that is not Jesus' way. Rather, he is with us as a fellow traveller on the journey through the storms of life, calming our frenzied anxieties and enabling us to have faith-filled trust in a caring father. Such is his gift to us if we are open to cry out for it and to accept it.

Thirteenth Sunday in Ordinary Time

Mk 5:21-43

To take health for granted is to be guilty of the greatest arrogance. To fail to thank God each day for the health one has is the crime of the unreflective heart. Our culture is becoming more and more health conscious. Propaganda constantly bombards us about a more healthy lifestyle. Some of this propaganda is true undoubtedly, but often the starting point is erroneous. It suggests that good health is something that we can accomplish entirely by ourselves. Not so, as the initial gift comes from God, the creator. The more we appreciate the gift, the better care we take of it and enjoy its wonder. Often, it is only when the gift is endangered that we turn to God.

When Jairus found his daughter sick unto death, as we hear in today's gospel, he turned to Jesus whom he had heard was a great healer. Even though his plea seemed to be too late, Jesus restored the girl to life and to her family.

Not all our prayers for the sick are so readily answered. However, our faith is that God cares for us totally in sickness and in health. It is his wish that we should storm heaven with prayer for the sick. Our prayer adds nothing to God's greatness but makes us grow in his love, in faith in his friendship. That friendship is a gift greater than health itself, greater than life. Such friendship is the only answer to our deepest yearnings in this life and the next. It is offered to all who make space in their hearts to accept it.

Fourteenth Sunday in Ordinary Time

Mk 6:1-6

Elections have interested me for over forty years. The recent local elections evoked joy and disappointment. The joy was twofold. I was pleased to see past pupils of mine take their place in the service of the community as elected representatives, and it was reassuring to find many mature campaigners of excellent calibre returned so convincingly. I wish them well. One of the disappointments of election times is to see some possible candidates of good merit rejected by the political machine because they have differed conscientiously with some aspect of establishment policy within the party. Expediency can become the criterion of selection rather than integrity or competence. It is nothing new, of course, to have somebody rejected for having the courage to stand up for what he believes is right, especially when it does not coincide with the popular view of the day. It happened to Christ himself as we hear in today's gospel. He went home to Nazareth where the locals were embarrassed by his goodness, felt uncomfortable with his preaching and were threatened by his lifestyle. So they sneered at his background and more or less pushed him out of town. His neighbours and those he grew up with rejected his goodness and all that he stood for. We can all be guilty of a similar rejection of anyone who challenges our complacency.

Fifteenth Sunday in Ordinary Time

Mk 6:7-13

Enjoying a fabulous site overlooking Cork Harbour, magnificent Cobh Cathedral was a landmark for generations of Irish emigrants to Britain and the USA. For many it was their last visual memory of the homeland as they set out in search of a worthwhile and fulfilling life overseas. Often, though poor materially, they brought with them resilient hope in themselves and tenacious faith in Jesus and in his church. Despite the odds against them, their hope bore fruit in the successful niches they carved out for themselves and for their families. Their faith was the bedrock on which numerous parishes and dioceses were built in many lands. The young sent out from Cobh enriched both society and the church worldwide.

Recently, Cobh Cathedral was the venue for another kind of sending out as five young men were ordained to priesthood. Like the disciples in today's gospel, these newly ordained are sent to create an awareness of God's presence in every aspect of life and of his focused presence in the sacraments, especially in Eucharist and Reconciliation.

Like the emigrants, these priests will need resilient hope and tenacious faith. These gifts of God are nurtured by their own prayer and by our prayer for them. As in all times of great upheaval and uncertainty, our times need apostles of faith and hope flowering in loving service. Our prayer this weekend could be that God will inspire each of us, and especially the young, to be apostles of Jesus wherever we go or wherever we are sent.

Sixteenth Sunday in Ordinary Time

Mk 6:30-34

The Samaritans assure us that they are always there to listen to anyone who wants to talk to them. To listen respectfully and sincerely to another is to bestow a blessing beyond compare. To be listened to reaffirms our self worth. It releases tension, eases stress, and helps to put life's problems and opportunities into perspective. Everybody needs an ear just as everybody needs to be a listener. But genuine listening demands a high price. It demands full attention, ruling out everything that disrupts focusing on the central issue of the moment. Some people are so insecure that often they talk incessantly about their own preoccupation and are unwilling or unable to listen. But it is through listening that relationships begin, friendships grow and love blossoms.

This is as true of our relationship with God as it is with one another. Anybody who is unable or unwilling to listen to a brother or sister in need of an ear, will be incapable of praying. Praying is listening to God and being listened to by him. Such listening needs space, a freedom from noise, distraction and television so as to focus on God and the things of God.

Things were no different at the time of Jesus as we hear in today's gospel. The disciples were successfully busy about the work of God, but Jesus takes them aside to concentrate on God himself. The gospel reminds us that our need of God is no less today, but if we really wish to hear him, we must create a sacred time space for him everyday. We can manage to do it for almost everything else. The choice is ours.

Seventeenth Sunday in Ordinary Time

Jn 6:1-15

To our way of looking at things, today's gospel has a fascinating climax to a miracle story. Starting off with five barley loaves and two fish, Jesus had just fed thousands of hungry people. They were so impressed they wanted to make him king. But Jesus' first thought was about the food that was left over. He asked his disciples to see to it so that nothing was wasted. His concern was all the more significant as we must presume that he could have fed twice as many if they were there.

His approach is a stark reminder to us in our time that all God's gifts are precious and must never be wasted. Yet, living as we do in the age of the disposable, we see enormous waste of food, clothing, energy, paper, glass, metal, plastic and of almost every resource that makes our lifestyle possible. Our waste makes life impossible for others. A less extravagant lifestyle on our part could make life bearable for many.

We are aware of the waste but we ignore its most obvious consequences, or rather, we think of them as somebody else's responsibility. But all human beings are made to be caring stewards of God's creation rather than marauding exploiters of its wealth. Human inventiveness is designed to enhance the earth rather than to destroy it.

Followers of Jesus have a special responsibility in this regard as he entrusts unto us not only material creation but himself in the Eucharist. If we fail to reverence his material gifts, we will probably fail to reverence the donor. Reverence for creation leads to reverence for the creator. The reverse is also true.

Eighteenth Sunday in Ordinary Time

Jn 6:24-35

Many of us are adept at misconstruing a situation when we choose to do so. The contemporaries of Jesus were no different as we hear in today's gospel. Having fed the five thousand, Jesus asked them to truly believe in him as the one sent by God but they argued that he would have to match the power of Moses whom they knew to be a messenger from God and who had fed their ancestors with manna over years in the desert.

Jesus was offering something much more precious than bread. They turned it into an argument. He was willing to fill the void in their empty hearts but they continued to focus on their hungry stomachs. He was inviting a response in friendship but they insisted on proof of power. Tormented by jealousy about his popularity, they refused to accept and appreciate the friendship Jesus offered. Instead, they wallowed in over-anxious testing of his credentials and missed out on the glorious reality that was on offer. It can happen to anyone of us. There can be no proof of love for the one who does not risk receiving love and responding to it. Faith in another is the foundation of all friendship, human and divine. It is on offer to us as much as it was to the Jews, if we are open to receive it. Perhaps, we would rather insist on proof.

Nineteenth Sunday in Ordinary Time

Jn 6:41-51

The command of Jesus, 'Do this in memory or me' is the focus and challenge of every Eucharist. It is the command to repeat the ritual of the Last Supper where Jesus becomes really present under the form of bread and wine. It is this but it is more, as we are reminded in today's gospel where Jesus unequivocally says that the bread which he gives is his flesh for the life of the world. He is giving his total self for the good of all people and his challenge to us and all his followers is to do the same.

The social consequences of the Eucharist are enormous. True, there is a precious personal privilege of receiving Jesus, but the call to imitate him through self-giving is also unmistakable. The danger is that we sometimes separate devotion from dedication, faith from fidelity, prayer from practice, the practice of justice, service and care. Some receive for themselves alone. Others give themselves heroically to others without receiving Jesus. Both are impoverished. Our receiving consumes Jesus. Our giving consumes us. The receiving gives us a share in the life of God. Our self-giving makes the love of God tangible in the world.

Respect for the Lord must mean respect for his brothers and sisters, especially the most disrespected of them, for we are all the Body of Christ. We must all be given the life of the world. It is truly an awesome vocation.

Twentieth Sunday in Ordinary Time

Jn 6:51-58

More people are living longer. The search for long-term security grows more intense among the presently financially secure. Others are so hard-pressed to survive that they can hardly look beyond next month. As well there are those, rich and poor and mainly young, who feel that employment uncertainty, marriage breakdown, pollution of air and water, drug culture, the nuclear threat, violence and genocide all make life so uncertain that the only thing on offer is the here and now, and the gratification of whim and desire immediately, no matter what the consequences. For all these groups today's gospel has a strong and definite message. There is life after death, and Jesus has left us a sure and certain pledge of that future glory in his own Body and Blood. The Eucharist is a constant reminder that we have not here a lasting home but seek one that is to come.

In ancient Ireland, a victorious chieftain often insisted that the son of a defeated neighbour came to live in his household as a pledge or guarantee of the vanquished one's loyalty. In his dealings with us, the Almighty God does things much more magnanimously. He gives us his Son in the Eucharist as a guarantee that he will fulfil his promise to bring us one day to eternal life. Nobody could have given a better pledge.

The invitation is to receive and to consume that gift totally so that as we become what we consume we are ready to receive the fullness of God's love in heaven. The Eucharist is truly an awesome pledge.

Twenty-first Sunday in Ordinary Time

Jn 6:60-69

Faith is like a fragile seedling. It may grow to blossom or it may so easily die. It was so from Jesus' own time, as we read in today's gospel. The crowds had seen his miracles but when they heard the promise of the Eucharist, they turned away. They just could not take on board such a reality. It offered too much and demanded too much. The offer was a sharing in the life of God himself. The demand was to live out the love and the values of the God who comes to change us. The offer and the demand were inextricably linked so the crowds rejected them both and walked away. Under the leadership of Peter, the seedling faith of the core disciples was protected. It grew and eventually blossomed into full commitment in the infant church.

In our time, many young adults and some not so young, are voting with their feet. They no longer come to Eucharist. It is true that they are also walking away from many other traditional institutions and values. But changing attitudes towards the Eucharist are much more significant because Eucharist is central to living as a follower of Jesus.

The incipient faith of the young is quickly crushed unless it is protected and nurtured. Who will speak the word of encouragement like Peter that will enable them to stay in the church and to blossom to full disciples? Can you do so? Will you?

Twenty-second Sunday in Ordinary Time

Mk 7:1-8, 14-15, 21-23

People are usually judged by how they live rather than by their ideals. Many people have had an ideal of a more just and caring society. Some work for it in a peaceful and self-sacrificing way. Others see violence as the way forward. For more people, talk about such an ideal is just ritualistic window dressing and they are not prepared to change their lifestyles to bring it about. Lip service is the only service they pay to their acknowledged ideal.

As we hear in today's gospel, Christ used his strongest language to denounce the Pharisees who proclaimed total service of the one true God as their ideal but who reduced that service to ritualistic washings and ceremonials which they called religion. Christ denounced their lip service and challenged them and us to a conversion of heart that would root out avarice, slander, adultery, deceit and every other evil that harms the neighbour.

True enough, we need our ideals. Christianity is built on ideals. They inspire us to better living, remembering that good is only achieved at great cost to those who do it and that when we fail, Christ is with us to enable us to begin again to strive for our ideals rather than settling for the lip service of mediocrity.

Twenty-third Sunday in Ordinary Time

Mk 7:31-37

We buried Martin Joseph in the bleak graveyard on the windswept hillside. We were glad to get back to the house for a hot cup of tea or a drink. There were many memories of the dead man shared.

A priest home from the USA recalled the encouraging words Martin Joseph had spoken the day he himself had left home for the seminary over fifty years ago.

A young widow assured us that she would always treasure the supportive advice the deceased had given her during her days of trial and loneliness. His own children and their children recounted his words of affection and respect, of firm but gentle rebuke, of friendship and of faith, of wise encouragement and reassuring challenge.

The neighbours, the publican, the local teacher, the postman, the nurse who cared for him, indeed, everybody in the house seemed to have been enriched by what he had said. Nobody remembered a harsh word from him, much less a lie, a calumny or a destructive criticism.

It gradually dawned on me what an inspiring use Martin Joseph had made of God's gift of speech. In today's gospel we find Jesus giving back to the dumb man the ability to talk. It is a gift that God gives to most of us each day.

Twenty-fourth Sunday in Ordinary Time

Mk 8:27-35

It is the crunch question for each of us as it was for Peter. Jesus asked: 'Who do you say I am?' Peter's answer was clearcut. 'You are the Christ.' For Peter, Jesus was the long awaited messenger, leader, saviour, messiah, sent by God to lead his people to the fullness of freedom. Slowly coming to know Jesus, Peter gradually accepted the consequences of realising who he really was and Peter lived the rest of his life accordingly.

Whether we listen to today's gospel or choose to ignore it, Jesus asks the same question of you and of me. In our inner hearts, who do we say Jesus is? One answer is that he was a Jew, a wandering preacher, a wonder worker, founder of a great religion, who is dead and gone. Another answer is that he was and is much more; that he walked a lone path to death, abandoned apparently even by God; that he rose from the dead and lives among us in the church, his people; that he is especially present to us in word and sacrament in the Eucharist and in the service of our needy brother and sister.

Which answer do we give inwardly to ourselves? Which answer do we live out in the routine of our daily lives? The deepening realisation of who Jesus is gradually affects every fibre of our being. To block that realisation is to reject God.

Twenty-fifth Sunday in Ordinary Time

Mk 9:30-37

It all seems so petty. The disciples of Jesus saw him as one who would free the country from the occupying Roman forces. After the revolution, they would be well in with the new boss. They could look forward to being better off than they could ever have expected.

Still, they were not satisfied. Each one wanted not only to be better off, but to be better off than anybody else, to be number one in the world's eyes. Their bickering led to Christ losing his cool with them.

He set about teaching once more that his way was different. To show how different, we find him in today's gospel, contrasting a child's trust with their adult status-seeking. It is a message that is as relevant today as in Christ's own time.

Christ's way is to do his Father's will, to do what he knows to be right, to be of service to those who deserve it and those who do not deserve it. His way is to serve whether he receives reward and recognition or rebuke and rejection.

Christ invites us to follow his way. It led him to death but, through it, to glorious resurrection finally. His way will lead each of us to the pain-filled death of selfishness and to the glory of love.

Are we willing to follow his way?

Twenty-sixth Sunday in Ordinary Time

Mk 9:38-43, 45, 47-48

Free offers are a growing feature of modern marketing. Some are of the three-for-the-price-of-two variety. Others seem to be saying that this product or service on its own is poor value but the extra free gift makes it nearly worth the money. A few offers are genuinely free to whet our appetites and to entice our future custom. The drug pushers find this latter approach most effective.

Overall, a great deal of modern marketing is aimed to seduce us into wanting what we do not need and what we cannot reasonably afford anyway.

One result has been to create an ethos that effects us all. It suggests subtly that there are free goodies in life for those cute enough to take them. That is a lie. Somebody always pays and rarely enough does anybody pay somebody else's share unconditionally.

Today's gospel is more honest and challenging. While it reminds us that the simplest kindness to a neighbour will be rewarded, it states bluntly and somewhat harshly to our ears, that accepting the love of God demands the ongoing elimination of selfishness and sin from our lives.

Religious practice can sometimes be polluted by the free offers mania creating a comfortable cocoon where we insulate ourselves from the radicalness of the call of Jesus. All love demands surrender. What surrender does the love of Jesus ask of me today?

Twenty-seventh Sunday in Ordinary Time

Mk 10:2-16

Today's gospel may evoke pain, anger, disappointment, condemnation, understanding, reassurance, hope, commitment. Whatever the immediate reaction, everybody has a vested interest in the critical issue of the teaching of Jesus on marriage, divorce and remarriage. The most futile reaction to this gospel would be one of blame. It is easy to blame. It is common to blame the media, educators, parents, preachers, partners or even God for the pain that arises from marriage breakdown. The real tragedy of our time is not so much that some people separate because, unfortunately, they find that they can no longer live together, but that so many forces in modern society contribute to the disintegration of marriage as a permanent commitment.

The Christian response is to build on what is worthwhile rather than to indulge oneself with negative criticisms that lead only to frustration.

Jesus puts God's plan clearly before us. It is that man and woman will be willing and able to commit themselves to one another for life. It is a plan that is worthy of our highest human calling. Everything that contributes toward its fulfilment is to be welcomed.

A constructive reaction to this gospel is to search for ways to strengthen family at home, at work and in the neighbourhood. Is there a selfishness or self-righteousness that needs to be tackled? Is there an opportunity to help the young that should be seized? Is there a group that enables truly loving relationships develop that should be, could be, supported?

The Christian calling is not to curse the darkness but to light candles of hope for the young and for the not so young.

Twenty-eighth Sunday in Ordinary Time

Mk 10:17-30

Questions are more important than answers. Questions involve uncertainty and pain but also lead to the ongoing search and growth which are the core of purposeful human living until we finally rest in God. Answers often lead to sterile stagnation and self-righteous security unless they lead to new questions that stimulate a thirst for an ever deepening appreciation of creation and its creator. To cease questioning is to be impoverished forever.

Questions sometimes led to inspiration, affirmation or challenge. Questions often lead to the unexpected. This happens in today's gospel when the young man tests Jesus about how to attain eternal life. This rich heir had kept the commandments faithfully always and, maybe, he was only looking for reassurance that he was doing fine. But Jesus seized the opportunity to invite him to greater friendship and intimacy with himself. The questioner turned down his chance and went away sad forever.

It can happen to any of us. We query God about why he allows world hunger. In reply, he challenges us to live more simply so that others may simply live. We try fudging the question because we do not like the clarity of his answer.

The questions we ask show the sincerity of our lives only when we are prepared to come and follow the Lord in whatever way he invites.

Twenty-ninth Sunday in Ordinary Time

Mk 10:35-45

Parents are always looking out for what is best for their children. The wife of Zebedee was no exception. She had two sons among the disciples. James seems to have been one of the senior members of the group and well respected. John was greatly in favour with the Master. The mother thought it best not to leave anything to chance. She would get a guarantee from the Master that her two boys would have the top jobs when the government changed. She believed in the direct approach. She sent the two boys to make a blunt request. The refusal was equally blunt. Jesus pointed out that anxiety for security and success was blinding them to what was best in the long term.

Something similar can happen today. Parents may foster ambition, self-indulgence, greed in their children. The gospel reminds all of us that what brings happiness, especially to the young, is the ability and willingness to be co-operative rather than competitive, to give rather than to accumulate, to care for others rather than be pampered, to risk security in order to serve. James and John and their mother are not the only ones who fail to heed his message.

Thirtieth Sunday in Ordinary Time

Mk 10:46-52

On every side, we are assailed by unrelenting and subtle advertising. It is designed to awaken insatiable longings for more comfort, enjoyment and security. It fosters the belief that having an ever widening range of indiscriminate experiences and products will bring inner happiness and peace. Such advertising works on the premise that the more one has, the more one wants. It abhors the wisdom that suggests that curbing selfishness frees one for true love and that possessions often blind us to our more basic needs.

Possessions were no problem to Bartimaeus in today's gospel. He did not have any, other than his cloak. He was poor and blind, a distressing and limiting combination. But he was clear on what was his greatest need. It was to be able to see again. He knew the value of what he had lost and he wanted it back. His plea to Jesus was unequivocal. 'Lord, let me see again'. He abandoned all his possessions, his cloak, in his urgency to put his case before the Master. He was not disappointed.

Jesus asks us the same question through today's gospel. 'What do you want me to do for you?' Are we clear on our first priority? With so many attractive or distracting options around, the essential can easily be obscured. Now is an opportunity to clear the confusion, to be ready to take up the Jesus offer, abandoning fear and selfishness. If we do so like Bartimaeus, we will not be disappointed.

Thirty-first Sunday in Ordinary Time

Mk 12:28-34

Nothing is as powerful as love. It is the powerhouse of all happiness, development and peace. It is never fully understood, explained or rationalised but it can transform the hearts of those who allow themselves to experience it. God loves each one of us uniquely, totally and forever. His love never changes. No matter how we fail to serve him, his love is constant. What does change is how we can appreciate and respond to such love. Sometimes we ignore it or reject it but even then we can never destroy it. We can grow in awe at the wonder of this mystery and allow it to change us, to mould us and enrich us daily. This is the core of the message Jesus brought us.

In today's gospel Jesus spells out the consequences of really believing this central fact of our faith and allowing it to influence the fabric of our being. The first consequence is that we will love God with an energising, consuming and joyful commitment. The second consequence challenges us to love each other as we love our own self. This self-love is built on a realisation that being precious in God's eyes, we must be precious in our own. God made us what we are. He enjoys his handiwork and loves it. So should we. It is as simple as that and as wonderful.

Thirty-second Sunday in Ordinary Time

Mk 12:38-44

Calculated cuteness is often the hallmark of comfortable religious practice. A common attitude is to do what seems essential for salvation and to leave the heroics to the saints. Religion and recklessness are rarely linked in our minds. Yet, religion without recklessness is impotent. The fact is that God, in sending his Son to save us, was quite reckless. If he had calculated the odds on our making an appropriate response to the gift of his Son, he would never have sent him. But his love far surpassed cautious self-interest. Jesus emptied himself of glory, taking the form of a servant. His giving of himself was total and unconditional, but open to evoke a response beyond our imagining.

Such giving is mirrored in today's gospel where the widow gave all she had, two small coins, less than a farthing. She could have given just one coin and kept the other as some little security against the rainy day. But, not so. Her giving was total, reckless, inspired by love. Her giving is remembered centuries later and is used by Jesus to inspire heroic surrender among his followers.

There is often some area of life that we refuse to surrender to the Lord. We hold on to some selfish security as a comfort blanket against the day of trial. Today's gospel is an invitation to reckless surrender of everything to the Lord.

Thirty-third Sunday in Ordinary Time

Mk 13:24-32

I seem sure that there will be a tomorrow, at least, for me. Indeed, I am putting some things off until then. In fact, I am planning for next year and the year after. It seems that to live fully, we must look to the future. Such forward looking hopefulness is central to much of our happiness and, yet, it is fraught with danger. The danger is that in looking to the future, we fail to fully appreciate the present and we trivialise the gift of this day. What we have is now, the precious minutes of today. How we use them shows whether we really know their value or not. Now is the God-given opportunity to grow in his love and in the service of the neighbour. It is unique and irreplaceable and will never come again.

Today's gospel uses dramatic images to depict the end of the world. Our own departure will be less dramatic but no less decisive. Our happiness in the future will be determined by our appreciation of the present. The suggestion is that we live each day in joyful hope as if it were to be our last on earth. Some such day will be.

Our Lord Jesus Christ, Universal King

(Thirty-fourth Sunday in Ordinary Time)

Jn 18:33-37

Change is a fact of life. The rate of change continues to accelerate. While urban renewal is changing the face of many towns and cities, much more influential changes are happening in the world of work, of technology, of education and in attitudes towards social life, relationships, family structures, moral values and religious practice. Perhaps the most profound change of all is in how the young of today are being formed in our world.

Change brings new opportunities for those who seize them and new burdens for those who find it difficult to adapt. Change is unsettling for everyone. Some find certainty in the tested ways of past generations, and credit the established norms with a life-giving certitude they never had. Such ill-founded security often blossoms into intolerant fundamentalism that uncharitably attacks everyone who, tentatively and in good faith, searches for new ways to live the gospel in such rapidly-changing circumstances.

In the midst of such turmoil, wise and innovative leaders are a blessing to be sought after and encouraged. Genuine leaders bind people together into respect-filled communities, where truth is a foundation stone, limitation is accepted, generosity is nurtured, love thrives and where uniqueness is more important than usefulness and charity is more precious than rectitude. More than anything else, the young need to experience such communities and such leaders, at home, at school, and at play. Christ the King is the role model for such leadership. He experienced rejection but he built a faith community. Nobody can do more.

St Patrick's Day

Lk 10:1-12, 17-20

It is often a crisis that brings out a person's full potential. In our time, some people have responded to the crisis of redundancy with ideas and courage in creating new jobs for themselves and for others. True enough, it is the blow of unemployment that evokes this response but there must be something in their background that gives people the strength for the challenge. It may be a supportive spouse, a resourceful parent, an inspiring teacher or an encouraging youth leader whose spirit sows seeds of commitment to an idea or to an ideal in another's heart.

For St Patrick, the crisis was exile into slavery. The strength was a spirit of faith that led him to pray constantly during the long nights on the job of minding pigs and cattle. The ideal to which he committed himself was to bring Jesus to a people who did not know him.

Rapid change in communications, in our understanding of authority, in work opportunities, in commitment to relationships, in sexual behaviour, has left our church in crisis. The quality of the response to this crisis is crucial. The belief that God is with us is the sure foundation on which to build a new vision. The vision must be to bring to birth cells of believers who will bring people to an awareness of God in daily life. Crisis is the opportunity to develop new wine-skins, new ways of being church, to embody today's faith as Patrick did so fruitfully in his time throughout our land.

The Assumption of the Blessed Virgin Mary

Lk 1:39-56

The true character of a man is often revealed in how he treats his mother, especially when he has done well in life himself.

Almost every man expects his mother to stand by him in a crisis situation. Such an expectation is well founded. The courageous and generous fidelity of mothers towards their sons in trouble is well proven. Mary was part of this great tradition when she stood by her son while he was being executed as a criminal on Calvary. To witness an execution is always difficult but the crucifixion of an innocent and only son must have been horrendous for a widowed mother. However, she was there and stood by her boy until the end.

But it was not the end. A glorious resurrection and ascension followed for him. When Jesus returned to his Father, it seemed to be the most natural thing in the world that he would bring his mother there. It was the least that would be expected from a man of his calibre. This is the feast we celebrate today, the Assumption of Mary, body and soul into heaven. On Calvary, Jesus gave Mary to us as our mother, so we have a share in her glory today as we have an assurance of her unfailing intercessory motherhood in the trials of every day.

Mission Sunday

Mk 1:35-45

During urban upheaval, the persistent banging of metal containers has long been a warning signal that some unwelcome presence is approaching. A crescendo marks its arrival. The rubbish bins of Belfast and Derry have clocked up years of effective service in spreading the word. Every society and group has devised ways to spread relevant news ranging from smoke signals to electronic pulses, from the pony express to E-mail, from magazines to encyclopaedias.

From the beginning, the followers of Jesus have always used every available means to spread the good news that God has taken flesh in Jesus and so has opened up the possibility of eternal life for all people. But in the Christian tradition the key means of spreading the word has always been and must always be the personal witness and the individual contact with believers reaching out to others and building up communities of faith in every neighbourhood.

Jesus himself set the example as he continually created opportunities to put people in contact with his Father and their Father. Peter and Paul took up the task and spread the gospel to Rome and many places in between. Even though it has blossomed and withered in different places at different times, the tradition has never died.

On Mission Sunday, we give thanks to God for the heroic generosity of our missionary brothers and sisters who spread the word worldwide through the example of their lives.

But the task of building God's kingdom cannot be delegated totally to missionaries, to priests or, indeed, to anybody else. Each of us who has been baptised has the responsibility and opportunity to build cells of caring, active believers who feed into the body of Christ and so make God's presence a tangible reality where we are. There is no substitute at home or abroad for the individual personal witness of the one who believes in Jesus and lives accordingly.

Will you help to build a community of faith in your parish this weekend?

All Saints

Mt 5:1-12

It is hard for us to imagine a life without a yesterday, a today and a tomorrow. The reason for our difficulty is that things are always changing for us. For the better, we hope, or for the worse, we fear. Our hopes and our fears so dominate our lives that they distract us greatly from the reality of the present. The reality is that God loves us each one of us totally, completely and forever. What makes a person a saint is that he or she realises this fact and becomes immersed in God's love. This happens permanently for a few in this life and for most people only after death. Then hopes are fulfilled and fears are wiped away. Yesterdays and tomorrows merge into a glorious present, filled with the presence of God. Today we celebrate the birthday into a new life of all who are experiencing the fullness of that happiness forever. It is the feast of All Saints.

And what of the Holy Souls tomorrow? A friend whose idea of perfect bliss was a good stand ticket at an All-Ireland final, used to liken the Holy Souls to fans who had secured excellent tickets but were slow to take their seats. They were secure but they needed a prod. It was a simplistic image but it helped him to pray for his loved ones who had gone before him. Even if his image does not appeal to us, we can follow his example of faith.

The Immaculate Conception

Lk 1:26-38

Opportunities taken and opportunities missed mark the life story of each one of us. Many a successful businessman spotted a niche in the market and, when the opportunity offered, he grasped it, thus setting himself up for years afterwards.

Others are rarely aware of their opportunities and even when they recognise one, they hesitate and the opportunity vanishes forever, leaving nothing but deep regrets behind.

One person who took her life opportunity with both hands and total commitment was Mary. Although she was only a young girl and apparently not yet ready for greatness or responsibility, she still grasped the opportunity God offered her and through her response changed the course of human history.

The core of this gospel is that Mary came to realise that God was asking for her co-operation in implementing his plan of salvation for humankind. Though unsure about how the plan could be accomplished, she trusted herself and her God sufficiently to commit herself totally to what he was asking. So God took flesh.

Jesus was conceived through the power of the Holy Spirit. The world was enriched irrevocably. Mary did not foresee the greatness of her call but her commitment ensured the fulfilment of God's plan. Mary's opportunity was unique but so is every opportunity God offers to each of us to participate in creating a better world where justice pervades, truth prospers, forgiveness abounds, trust matures, generosity grows, faith thrives, love inspires and hope is kept alive in every heart.

May we, like Mary, be over-shadowed by the Holy Spirit and bring the peace of Christ to our world.

Year C

First Sunday of Advent

Lk 21:25-28, 34-36

Water is the most precious natural resource any country can have. Valuable though oil, gold, uranium, forests may be, there is a growing realisation worldwide that water is a key element in all life and that the world's water resources are limited and being depleted. A few strengthening voices try to awaken public opinion to what is at stake.

On other planets where there is no water, there is no life. On this planet, this blessed resource is recklessly endangered through deforestation, radioactive waste and many other pollutants. In Africa, it is forecast that future political battles will not be about oil but about adequate supplies of plain water to sustain life. In this country we often bemoan the rains that ensure our abundance of some of the finest water in the world.

The familiar is so often taken for granted. It often takes a crisis to alert us to the fragility of life's treasures. Sometimes we ignore the warning signs and only appreciate a blessing when it has been taken from us through death or destruction, through carelessness or cowardice, through apathy or arrogance, through timidity or temerity.

Faith and family are two resource treasures that are endangered today. In a rapidly changing world, many of the civil laws and other conventions that supported both are disappearing. Destructive pollutants permeate every aspect of social living. We contribute to them ourselves through unprecedented self-centredness and irresponsible individualism.

Today's gospel challenges us to be more aware of the signs of the times, to realise how faith and family are being undermined. But it also reassures us that God will give us the strength to confidently survive all that is going to happen. Advent is a clarion call to protect and to nurture in our own lives and in society at large, the most precious gift God has given us. It is a call we ignore at our peril.

Second Sunday of Advent

Lk 3:1-6

Election campaigns too often degenerate into character assassinations. Past foolishness and failures are highlighted to discredit almost every candidate. The good they may have done is ignored and their errors are not only recalled but exaggerated out of context. In politics, there is little mercy for mistakes and there are few opportunities to make a fresh start.

In our relationship with God, things are very different. Though our sins may be scarlet, he is willing to make them white as snow. There is the constant invitation not only to make a fresh start but to begin a radically new way of living. No matter how selfish we may have been, he has shared our human nature to enable us to change direction and to move closer to his approach to living. Aware of how easily we postpone such radical conversion, the church offers us annual reminders of his coming to focus our hearts as well as our minds on his presence among us.

Advent is such an alerting and preparing time. Today's gospel is a timely reminder through the words of John the Baptist that Christmas is about more than food and drink, presents and pleasure, comfort and contentment. It is about preparing a way to let God have an ever increasing say in our lives.

In the hustle and bustle, will we hear his voice?

Third Sunday of Advent

Lk 3:10-18

John the Baptist must have been a powerful preacher. In today's gospel we find 'all the people', including tax collectors and soldiers, coming to ask him what they should do in order to be saved, to share in God's friendship. Of course, it was not his words that attracted people. From his frugal and committed lifestyle, they sensed that God was with him and they wanted to share in whatever it was that he had.

Things have not changed. People still hunger for God. They seek him here. They seek him there. Perhaps they lose heart. They do not see his influence at work in anybody's life. Where will they find him? How will they know the real thing? Through the lives of true disciples. 'By this will all people know that you are my disciples if you have love one for another.' 'Let the one who has two coats give to him who has none and the one with something to eat must do the same.'

Money talks. Genuine charity opens many a heart. Certainly its absence crushes the poor. Preaching alone never converts anybody. Making God's kingdom present on earth is every baptised person's privilege and responsibility. Advent is a reminder of our destiny.

Fourth Sunday of Advent

Lk 1:39-44

The history of the Jewish people has been better documented than that of almost any other race. It is a history studded with failure and glory, with disaster and revival, with betrayal and heroism. They were betrayed by their allies as well as by their own religious leaders. Yet the vision of who they were as God's chosen people, and of what he had in mind for them, never died. The Messiah was to be born of them. Every Jewish girl glimpsed the possibility that she might be mother of the promised one. However hesitatingly they believed in God, they trusted him to be with them, to be with them in their longings and in their near despair.

Certainly Mary believed and trusted not only at the annunciation, but right through to Calvary. Her early sufferings were triggered by uncertainty about Joseph's response to her pregnancy and by whispering about her unmarried status. The later agony was compounded through the betrayal of her son by religious leaders whom she had been reared to heed and to respect. They handed her son over to the occupying power to be executed. Such betrayal of trust was incomprehensible and it led to Calvary. But Mary never doubted that God was with her and would continue to be with her on the journey through life. She focused on his love for her and his kindness to her rather than on the human failures of those who represented him.

Her creative fidelity to God's word and her inspiring hopefulness in daily living have a particular relevance in our time.

Christmas Day

Lk 2:1-14

The Christmas travel trade shows clearly that we are still a nation of exiles. Travellers into Ireland will outnumber the outward departures by a hundred to one.

Thousands who live abroad by choice or by enforced circumstances will return to home and hearth for Christmas. Why will they come? It can hardly be for the weather or the prices. The reason is obviously deeper. It is the tie with their roots. It is a recognition that the family and place that give you life and form the fibre of your being are precious beyond counting.

Renewed contact with one's roots can be nurturing and refreshing. But we can forget the people and the traditions that made us what we are and what we can be. Maybe the exiles are more conscious of what Christmas is really about.

Christmas is about family, our own and God's. It is a reminder that Jesus has made a place for each one of us in God's family. We belong there now and always. It is reassuring to belong to his family. It means that he will never reject us.

In turn, we make a place of secure welcome for him and for one another in our human families, rejecting nobody and caring for all.

Family is about friendship, fidelity and the future. Friendship is the willingness to trust and to entrust, to trust the other person as oneself and to entrust oneself to others in security and freedom. Lived out each day, it is the foundation of family love.

Like all precious things, family and friendship must be protected. Fidelity is the bastion. It is the generosity to remain true to the fullness of love to which God has called us. While living fully in the present, family looks to the future with hope and confidence.

The hope is that the people and the values the family shares now will realise their full potential and always be cherished in the heart of the family. Without an eye to the future, family would be barren.

Jesus came to enrich our friendships, to strengthen our fidelity and to keep hope in the future alive. May he find a place in you and in your family and pour out upon you peace, love and joy.

Happy Christmas.

Holy Family

Lk 2:41-52

Alcohol is a many-faced creation. In some people it evokes relaxation, celebration and camaraderie; a gift of God for people's good. In others it leads to dependency and despondency, frustration and fear; abused through weakness or wilfulness.

Authority can have similar facets. For many it is a selfish power depriving us of our freedoms, restricting our whims or directing the course of our lives. Others experience it as a gift of God to protect, nurture and develop the precious things of life like genuine respect, uniqueness, friendship, fidelity, faith and true freedom.

In today's gospel we find Jesus returning to Nazareth to live under the authority of Mary and Joseph. The all-powerful one was to be under the authority of the village carpenter and his young wife. They had no power to compel him to do anything. He must have seen their authority as a gift from the Father to guide him in realising his true potential as a person. This authority was exercised in love and accepted in trust. Such is the authority that builds up individuals, family, community and the church itself.

Second Sunday After Christmas

Jn 1:1-18

On Christmas Day, the gospel story told of the birth of Jesus as a child of Mary. Today's gospel emphasises that Jesus is Son of God. It is obviously easier to describe his human birth and talk about his mother's people than to tussle with the mystery of one person of the Trinity taking on our human nature.

John the evangelist undertakes to lead us in faith into some deepening appreciation of this gift of God of himself to us. John uses 'the Word' to describe the person of Jesus who comes from the Father to live among us, one who has always existed but who at the moment of the incarnation begins a new human historic life among us.

It is only through him that we can know the Father, whom nobody has ever seen. In fact, it is only through Jesus that creation itself exists and that we can see and share in the glory of God.

Today's gospel is a proclamation of faith, intended to be heard and assented to rather than just read. It divides us into those who believe that Jesus is God and those who do not believe it.

Believers must make their own of this faith, express it through worship as well as lifestyle and acknowledge the wonder of a God who took flesh out of love for us.

Epiphany

Mt 2:1-12

Three wise men have taken on a new role in Irish society. Nearly intractable problems between political partners were entrusted for solution to three compromise explorers, popularly dubbed the wise men. There was an implication that in order to stay in power every difference could be covered over and every partnership could be held together by compromise no matter what principles or values were involved. The traditional wise men featured in the Epiphany gospel were made of sterner stuff.

For them principle was more precious than power, God's will more compelling than royal command. They rejected Herod's phoney interest in the new born king whom they were seeking so resolutely. They had grown in conviction about God's invitation to them to meet their saviour and they were prepared to endure hardship to follow whatever guidance God offered them. In their case, the guide was a star.

In our case, the invitation is the same but the guidance takes a different form. It is found in God's revelation of himself in the bible, in church teaching and in spirit-filled reflection on life experience. Like the star that disappeared occasionally from the sight of the travellers from the east, God's guidance is not always immediately obvious to us but it can be found through dedicated prayer within the community Jesus has left us in his church. What we need to bring to Jesus is not gold, frankincense or myrrh but listening hearts so that we may become truly wise in our search for God and for his action in our lives.

Baptism of the Lord

Lk 3:15-16, 21-22

In every community there are lone rangers as well as brothers and sisters. The lone rangers take part only in matters that are specifically in their own self-interest. They rarely row in behind ventures that benefit the wider community. Brothers and sisters tick differently. For them, the welfare of family members, neighbours, in-laws, colleagues and humankind everywhere is a core value. They know that individuals achieve fulfilment in life only by supporting what is good for others as well as for themselves. In this, they are following the example of Jesus as we hear in this weekend's gospel.

John the Baptist has called all the people of Israel to a repentance from sin expressed through immersion in the river Jordan. Being the sinless one, Jesus did not need such repentance himself but he recognised the need of his neighbours. He was fully part of his own people in their journey through life towards God. He knew where he belonged and he was happy to be fully part of it. His participation in the communal religious activity was rewarded by a new outpouring of the Spirit of God as he began his public ministry.

We live in an age of increasingly fashionable opting out of family, of neighbourhood, of parish unless there are immediate tangible benefits. Such individualistic opting out is the very opposite of Christianity. The loss is great on all sides. The need is to build an atmosphere where people will know in their hearts where they belong and be willing to participate fully in their heritage as communities of social living, of work, of worship and of play.

To take the initiative in building such life-giving cells is to give witness to Jesus. One fruitful New Year's resolution could be to develop and support creatively at every opportunity vibrant communal worship in our parishes.

Ash Wednesday

Mt 6:1-6, 16-18

There is an ever-increasing longing among us to choose the easy option, to eat, drink and be merry for tomorrow will never come. A strong strand in current advertising recommends that we enjoy now and pay later.

The message is both effective and insidious and touches all our lives in some way. Some of its effects are foolish rather than harmful but when such an attitude gradually permeates the fibre of our being and our society, the consequences are disastrous. It suggests that selfishness is the road to happiness and that comfort rather than God is our fulfilment. To follow such a philosophy of life is to live a lie. Living a lie is always destructive. It obscures the better option.

The better option is to live as Jesus would have us live, following the Father's will every hour of the day. That will asks that we concentrate on the preciousness of what makes us special to God rather than on the differences that separate us from each other. It requires that we love ourselves deeply so that loving others as we love ourselves evokes heroic generosity in us. It means that we live to the fullest the potential God has sown within us. Such an option gets very obscured in our world.

Lent is an opportunity to tone up for the struggle between settling for the comfort option and the transforming strength of Jesus option. Following Jesus brings a deepening peace that is open to all who walk with him through the self-denial and trusting generosity of Lent to the fullness of the Easter resurrection.

First Sunday of Lent

Lk 4:1-13

It is often suggested that each stage of a person's life is deeply influenced by a particular drive or instinct. While pride is ever-present in our hearts, the suggestion is that the young seek plea-sure, the middle-aged want power and the old put their hope in possessions. Some people find such wayward trends alive and well in every stage of their lives, and are happy in the ongoing human struggle by inviting Christ to be with them as they grow gradually in the gospel values that redirect these strong human drives.

Today's gospel recounts in a vividly descriptive way how Christ himself experienced similar temptations. The bread he was of-fered when he was hungry is a symbol of how easy it is to justify putting our own comfort and pleasure before the needs and rights of others. His trip to the high mountain with its offer of control over many kingdoms, alerts us to the many ways in which we can be tyrants in small ways through emotional black-mail in our families and through pressure groups on the job or in school.

The desire to be accepted and popular can be so strong that we are often tempted to do what will please rather than what is right, as happened to Christ on the parapet of the Temple.

In each situation, the choice is between selfishness and the other's good, between settling for human limitations or accept-ing our greatness as God's children. Lent is a time to strengthen the choice to belong enthusiastically to God's family.

Second Sunday of Lent

Lk 9:28-36

In order to grow, friendship needs space, sharing and trust. Time alone is not enough to build friendship. Some people can be work colleagues or neighbours for years without any real bond growing between them. Friendship can only grow where people make space in their lives for each other and use it to get to know each other, to share hopes, joys, fears and secrets, to trust the other person with what is deepest in oneself.

What was deepest in Jesus of Nazareth was his relationship with the Father. He was the beloved Son. Time and again, he went aside from the crowds to be alone with the Father in prayer. Oftentimes he took the apostles with him, especially Peter, James and John. With them he shared his fears about his future sufferings, his hopes of glory, but, above all else, his bond with the Father. One such occasion was on Mount Thabor where the trio glimpsed that their friend was the promised Messiah, the fulfilment of all their hopes. They had left their fishing behind to be with him. They had made space in their lives for his friendship and trust. He responded by strengthening their faith.

Today is our day for making space and time for Jesus in our lives. His response will always be generous. Today is Thabor Sunday.

Third Sunday of Lent

Lk 13:1-9

As one gets older, there is less hype about birthdays. The loved ones still share the happiness and the wider circle enjoy celebrating the major milestones. But as well as a sense of achievement, the reminder of advancing years has a sober side. For those with birthdays at this time of year especially, there can be a realisation that the number of Lents that is left to one is rapidly declining. As each year passes, there is one less opportunity to live through this season of faith, reconciliation, generosity, service, culminating in the Easter mystery. It is a season that is meant to bear fruit in our lives.

In today's gospel, Jesus tells us the chilling parable of the landowner who finds no fruit on his fig tree for the third year running. The tree looked well but was barren. The owner was disappointed and practical. He ordered it cut down. The gardener pleaded for a one year reprieve, one more opportunity to bear fruit. This Lent is one more opportunity from God to each of us to grow through prayer, through his word and sacraments, in appreciation of the wonder of the all holy God. He is the God who called Moses to lead his chosen people but who reminded him that contact with God is always sacred and he must be approached with reverential love. He is the giver of all good gifts and talents who enables us to bear fruit in fidelity, patience, kindness, forgiveness, courage and love. Otherwise, we may be just taking up the ground like the barren fig tree, admired by many but appreciated by none because of our failure to enrich our world as God meant us to do.

Fourth Sunday of Lent

Lk 15:1-3, 11-32

Life is a series of decisive moments strung together by daily routine and ongoing creativity. It is good to recall and to savour, if not always to celebrate, these key moments when the 'Yes' or the 'No', the 'I will' or the 'I will not,' the 'I'll stay' or the 'I'll leave,' changed our lives forever. Recognising and owning such moments awakens us to the realisation that the quality of daily life and of our lifestyle, as well as of our future, is sometimes much more under our control than we care to take responsibility for. Blaming others for the ills of our world, real and imaginary, is very often quite pointless. Being willing to choose the better option in every humdrum situation enables us to go for gold at the major decisive moments as they arise.

One of the great decisive moments in the gospel is in today's reading. 'I will leave this place and go to my father.' For the prodigal son, the past became irrelevant. The present took centre stage, opening up a new future. He broke free of chains of humiliation and guilt caused by earlier selfish mistakes. He trusted another, whom he knew had once loved him, to be loving enough to give him a fresh start. He trusted himself enough to take it. Often, it is this latter ingredient that is missing when we need to turn to our Father or to one another for forgiveness and reconciliation. Despite this hesitancy, we must never defer the opportunity to let go of selfishness, guilt or hurts and to be reconciled.

Lent is a key stage in our relationship with God. There is no doubting the offer of the Father's merciful reconciliation and the opportunity of new beginnings. It is the accepting or not of the offer that is our decision. The prodigal son decided wisely and came home to the one who loved him.

Fifth Sunday of Lent

Jn 8: 1-11

Labelling a person as a legitimate target is a nerve-racking tactic in present day violence. Whether it is a terrorist group fingering a lawyer or a building contractor, or whether it is a fundamentalist leader singling out a writer for execution, the fear aroused often evokes a sense of powerlessness in the community of the endangered person. Usually the labelled one is represented as a threat to some value that is important to the group who proffer execution as the best solution to protect their interest. Their authority to execute comes from their inner self-righteousness as guardians of what is good.

Similar groups were active in Christ's day as we read in today's gospel. The value to be protected was undoubtedly an excellent and essential one, the sacredness of marriage. Adultery clearly endangered it. The leaders of the mob were determined to stone the guilty woman to death, apparently to protect marriage, but really to wrong-foot Jesus before the people. It is easy to be delighted by how cleverly Jesus outwitted the self-righteous and to be encouraged by his mercy. But it is more sobering to realise how often we label people by our own careless gossip, and by our unreflective slander. We mean no harm, of course, but we still pass on the word, the rumour, the innuendo or the juicy scandal.

Execution horrifies us but character assassination is alive and well among us. To eradicate it from our lives would make us saints and make our families and communities oases of peace, joy and hope. To refuse to do so is to allow the cataract of self-righteousness to blind us forever.

Passion Sunday

Lk 22:14; 23:56

It is often said nowadays that the young know little about their religion and less about their faith. Sometimes adults are honest enough to admit that they are not much better off and unsure what to do about their ignorance. Next week, Holy Week, is one of the church's answers to the difficulty. For centuries, the liturgy of Holy Week has been directed to renewing faith, deepening love and awakening hope. Its purpose is to celebrate the passion, death and resurrection of Jesus, to hear and heed his teaching and to be enriched by the boundless generosity of his passion. The week's first passion story is in the Palm Sunday gospel.

This story touches each person in a different way as did the original experience. The centurion was doing a routine job, supervising the execution of a criminal. It seemed to be a soft number. The one to be executed was spun out already through the rough treatment the security forces had given him. His followers had run away. Despite the crowded streets slowing down the execution procession, he should be finished early and be able to get back to barracks for a long lazy afternoon. Then, it happened. He saw Jesus die and was convinced immediately and forever that here was a man of God. Peter, Pilate, Simon of Cyrene, soldiers, friends were all affected, each in his or her own way. For the centurion, a routine job had become a miracle of grace. For others, it remained just another execution.

Something similar will happen even among believers today and throughout the week. The experience will transform some, enrich many and leave others apparently untouched. But the mystery of the cross is that nobody is left unaffected by the passion story. The heart of every believer will be either enriched or hardened by Holy Week. The better option is available to everyone who is willing to stand at the foot of his cross this week and to be open to being convinced that Jesus is truly the Son of God.

Good Friday

Jn 18:1; 19:42

The memorial events marking the fiftieth anniversary of the liberation of Auschwitz reminded us again of the savagery that human beings inflict on one another. It is not that we need to delve into history for evidence of such brutality with ongoing wars and totalitarian regimes always developing more sophisticated techniques of human torture. What is new is that television now brings the experience of such depravity from all over the world into the heart of our homes, where sometimes there is great cruelty already. One danger is that familiarity makes us almost immune to the pain of this indescribable suffering. It also means that the sufferings of Jesus in his passion pale into insignificance by comparison with modern atrocities. But the core of the passion story of Jesus is not the intensity of his pain, intense though it was, but the person who endured the sufferings and the love that motivated him to do so.

The mystery is that an all-powerful God allowed the Son to suffer such a death at all. The explanation is the overwhelming love that the same God has for each one of us. On Good Friday, we ponder the mystery and we bask in the love. We realise that each one of us is so precious to Jesus that he actually died for us. The awesomeness of such love is both reassuring and challenging. It strengthens our confidence that all will be well for us in God's plan. It evokes a longing in us to live as the beloved family of such a loving God. We glory in the cross of our Lord, Jesus Christ.

Holy Saturday

Lk 24:1-12

The television programme 'Opportunity Knocks' has been the avenue to greatness for many stars. The time was right for them and they took their opportunity. If the TV had not come their way at that particular time, their whole life pattern would have been completely different. An important element on the road to greatness or to happiness is to be able to take a good opportunity when it offers itself.

Easter is a time of double opportunity. Firstly, it is a time to put the past right. Today is a day for reconciliation between man and God as well as between man and man. Often people need the impetus of the special occasion to get around to doing what they believe they should do. Of course, some people never renew their TV licences until the inspector knocks and then, it is too late. Secondly, Easter is a time to stride out with new confidence as a follower of Christ. It is an opportunity to let the power of God change fear into courage, hate into love, half-heartedness into generosity, even sinners into saints.

Maybe opportunity knocks for you today.

Easter Sunday

Jn 20:1-9

Tradition tells us that St Patrick lit the Easter fire on Slane, so highlighting for the pagan royalty at nearby Tara the central importance of the Easter mystery in the Christian faith. This faith was evoking a widespread and enriching response throughout the country even in Patrick's own lifetime.

Standing on Slane I reflected on how that faith has waxed and waned again and again throughout the centuries, spreading worldwide from this little island on the periphery of Europe. I wondered would Patrick see us now as an Easter people filled with joy in the Risen Lord and empowered by his spirit to live out the gospel.

Fire is both a powerful reality and an inspiring symbol. As well as being a source of light and heat, it refines and tests gold. It enflames what it touches. Even dying embers when brought together can release new flames, radiant with power and energy. Fire as a symbol of our faith challenges us to live as joyful apostles of the Risen Jesus, believing in his love and enabling his presence to transform our world.

This fire of faith must refine our values and test our lifestyles. It must inspire all those whose lives we touch and the society in which we live. The Easter candle is a symbol of the Risen Lord, the source of all our courage, hope and love. But we must not reduce the energising flame of faith to the flickering flame of a simple candle. Easter is a time to fan the flame of faith into an inferno that will burn away all fear and selfishness and enflame all hearts with love. Such is the vision. Easter people will not settle for less.

Second Sunday of Easter

Jn 20:19-31

Bargaining is part of life. Indeed it is a way of life for many. Some bargain about almost everything. To bargain is to focus on what we can get rather than on what we can give. It consolidates the cancer of self-centredness. Bargaining that is not mellowed by trust and generosity undermines self-respect, weakens friendship and destroys love. Indeed, it is only love that can move us from the anxiety of bargaining to the peace of self acceptance.

After the resurrection, Thomas was missing when the Risen Lord appeared. He was not impressed by the others' joy at meeting him. Thomas would not be convinced without proof. He would not easily entrust himself to another. He issued his bottom line for faith. 'Unless I see the holes that the nails made in his hands, and unless I can put my hand into his side, I refuse to believe.' It was strong talk. But then, the Lord appeared to Thomas and the bond of friendship between them melted the arrogance, took away the scepticism, cured the fear, and enabled Thomas to entrust himself totally to the Lord once more.

It is an experience that we need in our everyday relationships with each other and in our relationships with God.

Third Sunday of Easter

Jn 21:1-19

The distressing breaches of trust and the human failures of some in leadership roles in the church have caused great pain to many and sapped the morale and confidence of many more. One current temptation is to yearn for the more secure days of the past and to settle for safe religious practices to ensure one's own salvation, to avoid the challenging questions of the young, to retreat from proclaiming that Jesus is alive and well and still present powerfully among us through the gift of his church.

Such temptation also faced Peter and his companions. After the traumatic experience of the passion and the debacle of his own cowardice in denying the Master, and despite having met the Risen Lord, Peter was still so devastated that all he wanted to do was to go back to the fishing that had been the backbone of his life for so long. But Jesus came and called him out of himself again to show his love for the Lord by caring for his brothers and sisters by bringing them the good news of the Father's love. In ever-changing circumstances, Peter responded to the call generously and courageously. So must we. It is not a time for faint hearts. It is a time for a radical living of the gospel of justice, mercy, responsibility, service, fidelity and trust in the Lord. Such is our calling today, lay, religious and clergy. We must enable and support one another in responding to it.

Fourth Sunday of Easter

Jn 10:27-30

It was very late one night last week as I sat in the chapel in Maynooth College where I had prayed as a young school leaver thirty years ago. At that time I had visions of all I would achieve for Christ. I would maintain his flourishing church and build it to new heights. It was a time of great confidence and optimism. I thought that the important part of vocation was what I would do for Christ. Over the years, it has gradually dawned on me that the core of religious vocation is not what I do for him but what Christ offers me. His invitation is to intimate friendship, a friendship that yields a harvest in the service of the gospel.

The style of service has changed. The world and the church have changed radically in these last thirty years. The tussle for the minds and hearts of the young grows more challenging daily. The need for dedicated and competent frontline workers is greater than ever before. But the essence of Christ's call for his fulltime volunteers is still the same. It is a call to total commitment to his friendship and his service. In an uncertain and disillusioned world, it is much harder for the young to respond to a call to a permanent bond with the Lord. But the call is as certain as ever before.

Vocations Sunday is an attempt to create an awareness and an atmosphere of faith and support where that call may be heard and heeded by young people of courage, concern, confidence and conviction, who place their hands in Christ's with faith and love in their hearts.

Fifth Sunday of Easter

Jn 13:31-35

One opinion is that the first child in a family is often the quickest to be articulate because the parents constantly chat up their first arrival. Others might think that it may be a later child, the third perhaps, who progresses most rapidly as the elder two coax, cajole and encourage the younger one to repeat what they say.

Whatever about the differing opinions, the fact is that we develop our talents and skills, our attitudes and lifestyles, by imitating others. Imitation makes us what we are. Our uniqueness will later enable us to be creative, but firstly we are imitative.

To imitate Christ is to be Christian. To recognise his values, and to make them our own in how we live, is to be true to our destiny.

Today's gospel points out that the crucial imitation is to love the other person just as Jesus loved each of us first. His love knew no bounds. He forgave his executioners and he loves each of us as much as he loved them. Secure in that love, we must reach out to one another.

It is on this love that salvation is based, and not on private religious practices. The challenge is intimidating, but love of the neighbour is the identity badge by which the followers of Jesus will recognise each other and, in turn, be recognised by people everywhere.

For one's own long-term benefit, it is important always to carry this essential means of identification and to update it daily.

Sixth Sunday of Easter

Jn 14:23-29

Fear touches our lives in many ways. There is the fear of pain, hunger, illness, of being redundant, rejected or ridiculed. Often there is such a real basis for these fears that it would be foolhardy not to be anxious. But there is another fear, a personal inner fear that blocks one from accepting one's own goodness, from trusting the goodness of God or of other people. This is a fear that stops one reaching out with the act of kindness lest one appears to be a soft touch and so be exploited. It deadens the word of praise or good news even before it is voiced lest another be affirmed or encouraged. It postpones indefinitely the initial hug of forgiveness that could balm an aching heart and begin a deepening relationship. This fear ensures that a challenge to generosity, fidelity or truth is not uttered lest it transforms the heart of an individual, a family or a community. It traps an individual in the darkness of one's own self-centredness and limitations. It can show itself in defensiveness, arrogance or addiction. It destroys all joy in one's heart.

Today's gospel offers an escape from the web of fear that can entrap anyone. The escape route is the peace Christ promises to each one of us. To be healed of fear is Christ's gift to us. To enable another person to escape such fear is a cornerstone of the Christian's calling. It is the challenge facing God's people today.

Ascension Thursday

Lk 24:46-53

In urban areas especially, Thursdays are becoming very busy commercially, with the increasing volume of late night shopping. For many householders, Thursday is the most opportune time to stock up for the weekend and indeed for the full week ahead. In such an atmosphere, it is particularly difficult on a Thursday to focus our hearts and minds on any religious feast no matter how significant. So despite its centrality to our faith, Ascension Day is being ignored. While the loss is great we can lessen its impact by reflecting on how St Luke wrote about the event itself. Luke wrote both a gospel on the life of Jesus and a news report on the activities of the infant church. Ascension features as the finale to the gospel and as the opening of the Acts of the Apostles. Both accounts are complimentary in highlighting that an important state of the mission of Jesus was now complete and as he was returning to the Father, he was entrusting to the disciples, the young church, the ongoing task of preaching forgiveness in his name. To inspire them for this daunting task, he promised the ongoing presence of the Holy Spirit.

With the same promise, the same task is entrusted to us. It is to believe that Jesus died and rose from the dead so that all people could be reconciled with God and with each other. In the security of faith, we must bring such reconciliation to others by word and example so that, being gathered through baptism, all may worship him with joy. Through the gospel, we are to be a reconciling people wherever we are.

Seventh Sunday of Easter

Jn 17:20-26

I have always been encouraged and supported by people who pray for me. It was as a student for the priesthood that I first realised that a whole circle of neighbours and friends remembered me daily before God and still do. To them I say thanks. But I am even more reassured by today's gospel which tells me that Jesus himself prays for each one of us to his father. He prays that the love that the Father has for him will also be in us. Through this love, we are invited, encouraged, enabled and challenged to be just as united as the Father and Jesus are. It is through this unity in our families, in our parishes and in our schools that the young will come to know and accept that we are Christian.

Each family is called upon to be such a centre of care and respect for one another that the young will experience the Spirit of God living there.

When a parish is seen as a community of families where the need of one is the concern of all, the world will really know why Christ came. To be entitled to call itself Christian, a school must be a place where the belief that each one is a child of God results in a practical atmosphere of trust, harmony and partnership.

Ideals, yes. But Christ is praying that they will be reached. To follow him, we must be striving for them.

Today, we listen again to his prayer for us.

Pentecost Sunday

Jn 14:15, 16, 23-26

For many the church is in great disarray. Fewer people are taking part in services. A growing number seem to ignore its guiding teaching. The falling number of full-time personnel is causing heart-searching, if not panic, among church leaders and among the committed themselves.

The church is certainly in crisis. In some hearts there is a yearning for the securities of bygone days. But the church is an instrument of God's presence in the world, and in a world of ever-quickening change the church must be attuned to the contemporary situation so that the essential perennial values and power of Christ permeate everyday life in our time. To bring this about is the daunting task facing all of us who follow Christ.

It is the same task that faced the first disciples. Believing that they were under attack after Christ's departure, their initial response was to hole up in the upper room to protect themselves and their beliefs. Then came the magnificent outpourings of the Holy Spirit which we recall as the first Pentecost.

Filled with this Spirit, the once frightened disciples came out of their bolt hole with courageous abandon, preaching the Risen Christ and building caring communities of outgoing believers.

Fear-filled defensiveness was replaced by exuberant confidence as they realised Christ would turn every crisis into an opportunity to build his kingdom in ways that they would never have foreseen.

Today is an opportunity to pray for a similar outpouring of the Spirit into our lives so that the world may recognise us as believers who know that God always walks with his people and will never desert them.

Trinity Sunday

Jn 16:12-15

Like politicians, parish priests are the butt of many a story. One PP's habit of listening at the back of the church to the curate's sermons annoyed the younger man greatly. On Trinity Sunday, the curate exploded: 'My dear people, the Blessed Trinity is a mystery; you cannot understand it, I cannot understand it and the Canon down there behind the pillar cannot understand it either.'

Some of the listeners were not sure whether he was frustrated by the eavesdropping Canon or by the difficulty of preaching on the mystery of the Trinity.

The snag about mystery is that the emphasis has been wrongly placed. We have been constantly reminded that we cannot fully understand a mystery. But we can appreciate many aspects of it. Many a person cannot understand or explain a partner's love and personality but can experience it, appreciate it and respond to it when it is revealed.

The Trinity is what Jesus, God made man, has told us about the nature of God. He constantly speaks of the Creator as Abba, Father; one with whom he is completely united and yet, the one who sent him. Jesus promises us a helper, the Holy Spirit, God continuing to inspire and strengthen us. One writer described the Trinity as 'God's three ways of being there.'

Some of the best things in life are appreciated rather than understood. 'Glory to the Father, Son and Holy Spirit.'

The Body and Blood of Christ

Lk 9:11-17

Even though the story has often been retold, there is one very challenging line in this gospel. A huge crowd had followed Jesus and were now weak with hunger. The disciples were hungry too but before they opened up their own meagre supplies, they wanted the mob sent away. After all, the disciples had been far seeing enough to provide for themselves and they did not want to share their resources with the improvident. But Jesus was not co-operative. His command was clear. 'There is no need for them to go; give them something to eat yourselves.' It is a command that has resonated among Christ's followers over the centuries since. Everywhere the Eucharist is celebrated, the poor and the hungry are cared for, sometimes generously, sometimes less so.

Traditionally, we are a generous people but the temptation to selfishness is never far away and we live in a world whose first commandment is mind oneself. This gospel constantly reminds us that feeding the hungry, sheltering the homeless, caring for the less able is at the heart of following Jesus. Religious practice will not substitute for meals on wheels, for aid to Sudan, Bosnia or Romania, for Hearth or Shelter. To feed the hungry is to be truly a disciple of Jesus. It is our calling.

Second Sunday in Ordinary Time

Jn 2:1-12

As a youngster growing up in a public house, the miracle at the wedding feast of Cana made me feel uncomfortable. I felt that Jesus was unfair competition for the local licensed trade. Indeed, if he went on like that he would put all of us out of our jobs. It was one way of looking at the incident. There are other ways.

In simple human terms, Jesus did what he could to help his neighbours in their hour of need. It is an example worth following.

Of course, it was also a sign of who he was. He was the young man from Nazareth but he was more. He was the Messiah. God's chosen one, sent to set up God's kingdom on earth. Even before the miracle Mary obviously believed that he was special. However, it was only after they had seen his power in action that the disciples believed in him. With faith in herself and in him, Mary challenged the young Jesus to meet the need of the time and place. He responded, Mary saw the need. She risked rebuff and failure.

Without risk, nothing worthwhile is achieved. But for Mary, there would have been no miracle at Cana. How much good is left undone because nobody has the vision to see the other person's potential for good and to call it into action? As never before our society needs people of discernment and courage like Mary.

Third Sunday in Ordinary Time

Lk 1:1-4; 4:14-21

Today's news is tomorrow's history. News reporting is the seed-bed of history. Sometimes the reporter is present at the event. Other times, the report is based on interviews with those who have first-hand knowledge of what happened. St Luke did not come on the scene until some years after the life, death and resurrection of Jesus. But he was a painstaking and reliable reporter. He met and worked with many who had shared the life of Jesus and the apostles, possibly even meeting Mary who had been there before the crib and after the cross. From such sources, he gleaned accurate and full accounts of the life and teaching of Jesus. He put order on these stories to present Jesus as God who became human to show God's merciful forgiveness of all people.

As we hear Luke's gospel read on the coming Sundays, we realise that as well as being history, this gospel story is alive and life giving. It points up the links between us and Jesus. His work recounted in today's gospel is continued in the church through each one of us. Just as Jesus was anointed to bring good news to the poor, so each baptised follower is enabled by the Holy Spirit to give sight to those blinded by selfishness, to free those entrapped by guilt, to awaken hope in the downtrodden. To merely hear the gospel and not allow it to inspire one to a joyful living of its message is to ignore the nourishment our faith needs today. Faith is nurtured through gospel living. Undernourished faith quickly dies. Shared faith never dies.

Fourth Sunday in Ordinary Time

Lk 4:21-30

Peace is much more than the absence of violence. It involves mutual respect and acceptance of difference as well as the surrender of privilege and prejudice. Similarly, truth is much more than not telling lies. It permeates every aspect of our communication with each other. Indeed, truth is the life blood of all our relationships. It must affirm what is best as well as alerting us to the selfishness and the blindness that can endanger even the most precious things in our shared lives. Avoidance of lies is like an outer defence wall, necessary but sterile in itself. It forms a safe haven where our interpersonal relationships can take root. But they can only blossom and bear fruit in an atmosphere of open, sensitive and creative honesty. Such honesty in pointing out destructive failure to others can be very painful, especially when the recipients are locked into self-righteous security.

This is what happened in today's gospel. Jesus pointed out to contemporary Jewish religious leaders that they had failed to truly appreciate their heritage as children of God and that God's salvation is for all peoples. His listeners disliked the message and set about destroying the messenger. Yet, for Jesus to have remained silent would have been a cowardly failure to speak the truth. He spoke not to condemn but to point out a better way.

Sometimes, perhaps often, we lack his caring courage. We shield ourselves with self-deceptive layers of not hurting others or not interfering even when we know deep down that the truth is calling us to take the less travelled road. Yet such wise courage in truth is essential for the wellbeing of each family and association, in church and state. We all need to have such courage sometimes, even at the risk of being rejected. Good is only accomplished at great cost to those who do it.

Fifth Sunday in Ordinary Time

Lk 5:1-11

There is no end to how extraordinarily kind, caring and dedicated some people are to their neighbours at times of need. As well, there are many people who devote themselves tirelessly and unfailingly to community activities in workplaces, schools, sports clubs, political parties, parishes and churches to benefit very wide circles of people. Yet many other individuals never get involved personally in such activities. For some the reason is selfishness. Many others remain on the edge because they do not appreciate the difference their involvement would make to the community and to themselves. For some, though willing to serve, lack the self-confidence to overcome shyness, embarrassment, fear of rejection or whatever else prevents them from participating. Perhaps, they feel unable for the commitment however small or they see themselves as unworthy of the trust that community service involves. Their false humility cripples the stirrings of reaching out that awaken in their hearts.

Something similar almost happens in today's gospel. Through directing the fishermen disciples to huge catches of fish, Jesus, the carpenter from landlocked Nazareth, shows himself to be a man of great authority and power in the eyes of Simon Peter who feels totally unworthy to be his co-worker. Peter pleads to be allowed to return to his fishing which is what he knows best. But the reassuring words of Jesus enable him to step out beyond his own anxieties to share in the wider work of the seedling church. His courageous response changed the world. So can yours.

Sixth Sunday in Ordinary Time

Lk 6:17, 20-26

Lotto fidelity goes from strength to strength. Each week thousands of fans ensure that whether they are at home or away, in hospital or on holiday, they are in with a chance to become wealthy. Some arrange their social life, and even their religious worship, to enable them to see the actual selection of numbers on the television. Many say that they do not want to become millionaires really but that they would like to win enough to be more comfortable and better provided for.

It is said that those least able to afford the outlay are the more addicted. Their needs are certainly the more pressing but the fantasy that wealth in itself brings happiness touches most hearts at some level in our world today. The longing for a little more than we have can subtly grow into the most insidious cancer undermining true happiness.

In today's gospel, Jesus offers another option. He proposes that rather than freeing us, possessions often possess us, creating anxieties about security and awakening selfishness that cripple us. According to the beatitudes, the poor in spirit know the true value of all God's gifts so enabling us to live in a way that opens us to the joyful reception of his greatest gifts, life and love.

Such an attitude of mind and heart lends itself to developing the inner security that blossoms in generosity towards the hungry, in support for the oppressed, in sympathy with those who mourn, in mercy towards those who fail.

To choose the Jesus option daily is to reach joy through pain, happiness through love, friendship through prayer, security in God and in his people. It is the fundamental option.

Seventh Sunday in Ordinary Time

Lk 6:27-38

Decisions by the Federal Reserve Bank in the USA often seem to determine the rise in mortgage repayments for families here, while the influence of the German Bundesbank on our economic life and employment opportunities is similarly decisive. While these institutions bear no illwill to the rest of humankind, they see their primary responsibility as protecting the resources of their own countries and of moneyed people within them.

Today's gospel message of caring lovingly for one's neighbour has little effective meaning for them. Their vision of achievement is money well managed to make more money. Success is clearly measured in percentages and richly rewarded in kind. Failure is rarely forgiven and is often more enduring than the transient success of even the most successful.

There is another vision of greatness and glory where failure is always forgiven and success is immeasurable because it is known fully only to oneself, to God and to those who share intimately in it.

Such is the vision of Jesus for each of us. Its inspiration is love received, love shared, love in the heart, love in action, empowering love, sustaining love. It is knowing that we are loved unconditionally by God.

It is a challenging vision. It calls for greatness and perseverance of heart. Jesus never intended his followers to settle for mediocrity. Do we?

Eighth Sunday in Ordinary Time

Lk 6:39-45

Some people spot talent. Others spot weakness. Some see the best in people. Others are unhappy until they find something wrong with them. The former might be called optimists and the latter pessimists but the difference is more significant. One attitude sees people as individuals worthy of deep respect, each with a unique purpose in life, and precious in God's eyes. Secure in themselves as being loved by God, they can risk seeing others as loveable no matter what their limitations are. The other attitude is that of knockers who see every trait of goodness in another as a threat to themselves and so focus in on every vein of weakness. The knocker judges everybody as guilty until proven innocent and even then begrudges the benefit of the favourable verdict.

Such a judgemental attitude of heart evokes a very stern warning from Jesus in today's gospel. Those who set themselves up to judge others will be severely judged themselves. It is a caring God alerting us to the fact that intolerance of the weakness of others coarsens our hearts and makes us incapable of loving ourselves, others or God. Such a loss is worse than any adverse judgement.

Ninth Sunday in Ordinary Time

Lk 7:1-10

'Have you stopped beating your wife yet? Yes or No?' No matter which answer an innocent man gives, he stands condemned. The way the question is put limits the possibilities and rules out the possibility that the man has never beaten his wife. Something similar happens when one is asked: 'Do you think that God will change his mind and answer your request when you pray?' Obviously, God does not change his mind and so, the implication is that prayer of asking is a waste of time or worse. But that is not the only possibility. There are other ways of looking at our prayers of petition, our prayers for health, for joy, for love, for forgiveness, for strength, for a child, for justice, for grace, for wisdom. Our prayer adds nothing to God's greatness and knowledge. It is an expression of our dependence upon him. It triggers off within us a deepening awareness of his varied gifts, of the fact that everything is his gift. In God's plan, our asking is a key strand in his caring for us. Quite simply, we pray to God to meet our needs because that is how he wants it to be. Our prayer itself is good for us.

In today's gospel, we have the centurion, an outsider, asking Jesus to heal his servant. He even asks others to intervene on his behalf. He acknowledges his own unworthiness. His faith in Jesus is rewarded.

Things have not changed. Faith in the love and power of Jesus, expressed in prayer, is still an occasion when he reaches out to us, his chosen people.

Tenth Sunday in Ordinary Time

Lk 7:11-17

It was so casual. It often happens to many of us as well as to Jesus. He was just going down the road and met a funeral. It was coming out of Nain.

There was much grieving because an only son had died and the mother was a widow. There and then, on the spot, Jesus raised the dead man to life and restored him to his mother. It all seems so simple and matter of fact.

At tragic moments like the early death of the father or mother of a young family, many a person has wondered why God lets this tragic death happen. He was moved to pity at Nain.

Why not in Cork or Kerry? I still do not understand fully why God lets the cross so crushingly into some people's lives, but I do know that God continues to care for each of us no matter what the tragedy.

We would often want him to do that in a Nain-like way. But that is not his only way. His love and care do not end with death. Indeed, death is the gateway to closer life with him. For the bereaved, his care shows itself through the love and support of family, friends and neighbours. It is through us that he shows that care.

As we listen to the Nain story, let us be alert to our privilege of being co-workers with Jesus in caring for each other in time of death.

Eleventh Sunday in Ordinary Time

Lk 7:36-8:3

Accepting forgiveness is more important than giving it. Accepting it seems so easy to do. We feel that if only the other person would forgive, there would be no nurtured grievances or phantasised retaliations. But it is not as simple as that. To accept genuine forgiveness, one must admit to oneself and to another that one has failed. To accept forgiveness, one must first accept guilt. In our time, that is the crunch. Pride will not let us recognise our selfishness and if we do not admit our failure we can never accept forgiveness.

In today's gospel story, the adulterous woman makes no attempt to deny her wrongdoing and so is open to accept Jesus' forgiveness with the peace it brings. Something similar is operating in all our relationships with each other and with God. A cornerstone of happiness is to be able and willing to admit our failures as a prelude to accepting the healing power of genuine forgiveness. The proud can never do it. Self-righteousness is always a barrier to love.

Twelfth Sunday in Ordinary Time

Lk 9:18-24

In every heart is a struggle for supremacy between opposites. The longing to take revenge, or at least to nourish a grudge, struggles with the spirit of forgiveness. The need for peer approval undermines the courage to reach out in truth for what is right. The craving for pleasure nibbles away at the generosity that would share all with the less well off. Infatuation with the new and the novel does battle with the bulwark of fidelity. In every area, goodness demands a sacrifice. Good is only achieved at great cost to those who do it.

Jesus makes the point forcefully in today's gospel by challenging his disciples to renounce their selfish instincts if they wish to follow him. Jesus showed by life and death that there is no such thing as cheap love and that real commitment demands a surrender of one's own individualism in favour of the needs of all God's family. Just as there would be no streams, rivers or drinking water without the individual raindrops falling, so there can be no reservoir of generous love without our separate personal little acts of self-denial.

Thirteenth Sunday in Ordinary Time

Lk 9:51-62

On Monday last, a phone caller asked me if I had my reflections on today's gospel written yet. The reason for the query so early in the week was that the caller found this particular gospel very challenging and frightening. It shows Christ as a travelling man of no fixed abode, a man of no property with no place to lay his head. One man was willing to follow Christ later if he left an address where he could contact him. Christ's invitation was to come now, pronto. It is the same Christ who invites some to leave even their bereaved families to go and spread God's kingdom. It is the same Christ who demands that his followers keep their eyes set straight forward on the goal, God's will. Any looking back over one's shoulder to other gods like money, security or sensuality will bring dire results, just as the ploughman who works on rocky soil will be in trouble if he looks back at what he has ploughed rather than keeping his eye on what is still to be undertaken.

Each person's call is different and unique. But in a variety of ways, the gospel is saying that to follow Christ demands that we give up anything that keeps us back from following him. Is there any barrier between me and God? Today's command is to remove it today.

Fourteenth Sunday in Ordinary Time

Lk 10:1-12, 17-20

Few have it always. For some, it is the basic thrust of their lives. More enjoy it occasionally. Others seem to have never even glimpsed it. All are capable of receiving it. Everybody longs for this inner personal peace. Such peace is an experience that, limited though one is, each one is created to be totally loved by God and loved by others and, in response, one is capable of loving God, now and forever, and this love is fostered in and through human love and service. The cancer that endangers the harmony between what we are and what we aspire to be is a fear-filled anxious pride that blocks our receiving God's all-pervasive gift of peace.

A malaise of our time is to seek happiness in a self-centred independent security that denies both our creaturehood and our interdependence. We forget that we are made for God and for each other and not for ourselves alone. Contaminated by this malaise, we barricade ourselves in privacy and self-interest.

The antidote is to trust the Lord. Such trust is a gift of God, freely given to all willing to entrust themselves to him. Each Eucharist is an opportunity to do so. Today's gospel is a reminder to the followers of Jesus to build a world where such trust and peace can take root and flourish.

Fifteenth Sunday in Ordinary Time

Lk 10:25-37

Some gospel stories have become so absorbed into our psyche and so commonplace that oftentimes we only allow ourselves to be reassured by their familiarity rather than be challenged by their radicalness.

One such story is that of the good Samaritan. On the road from Jerusalem to Jericho, he was the only one to help the mugged traveller. His practical and generous kindness was commendable and will be ever remembered. But it was not the crucial point of the story. Jesus was much more anxious to confront the self-righteousness of his listeners rather than shame them into helping a neighbour in need, praiseworthy though such service could be. He saw clearly that the dry rot that bedevilled the religious people of his time was their continual preoccupation with their own understanding of God's law and their total dismissal of those who did not conform. So the Samaritans were written off. Yet it was one of them who left his own cares aside to help when the guardians of propriety passed by on the other side.

In our own day, it is so easy to apply this story to others. The real gospel gift is to allow the power of God's word not only to challenge us but to change us, remembering that self-righteousness is much more treacherous than selfishness.

Sixteenth Sunday in Ordinary Time

Lk 10:38-42

The milder weather makes life easier in some respects for the homeless, the housebound, the infirm and the deprived. On the other hand, it can be a very lonely and anxious time for the dependent, as the people who normally care for them take off on holidays. 'Who will care for me while they are gone?' is the unspoken fear in many a heart.

Today's gospel has Martha and Mary inviting one homeless man into their home for the evening meal. Even though it gave rise to some hassle, it was probably easy enough for them to do so as the man in question was respected and respectable. He was Jesus of Nazareth. Many of us would be happy enough to do the same and have him to dinner. This we can do, because he assures us that what we do to the least of our brothers and sisters, we do to him.

Will we care for him in any of our brothers and sisters this weekend?

Seventeenth Sunday in Ordinary Time

Lk 11:1-13

The familiar can quickly lose its impact and its power to enrich. The rugged splendour of a Kerry mountain may not evoke the same reaction in a local sheep farmer as in the awestruck first-time visitor from the lowlands of Holland. For one, the wonder of the scenery may be so overshadowed by the difficulty of eking out a living that it is not appreciated. For the other, the prospect of further panoramas stimulates an urgency to explore new territories.

A similar situation can happen in our relationship with God. Saying prayers can become so routine as to be barren and the cares of life can obliterate the wonder of creation. We lose contact with the creator and the source of inner peace dries up. To avoid such a loss, one must establish a daily oasis of time and space where one focuses one's life into a deepening friendship with the most wonderful parent who can be imagined, our God.

As we read in today's gospel, the disciples saw Jesus take the alternative approach. He went aside to pray to his Father. They were attracted by what they saw and asked to be taught to share in such an experience of prayer. Prayer is a gift but everybody can be taught to be open to it. The prayer of persistent asking is a good beginning but the prayer of thanksgiving and praise will transform the impoverished heart. Reflective recitation of the Lord's prayer can open up ever-enriching vistas of God's love for us. Lord, teach us to pray.

Eighteenth Sunday in Ordinary Time

Lk 12:13-21

As the cancer of unemployment wreaks havoc among so many communities and as the recession continues, the temptation grows to moan about how badly off we are. We seem to have inoculated ourselves against the pictures of famine-afflicted Somalia and war-scourged Bosnia as well as against the plight of homelessness at home. The worldwide problems of poverty and hunger are so overwhelming that they produce a sense of hopelessness and fear in us that can paralyse our generosity and our care for others.

Today's gospel is an antidote to this malaise. At first hearing, its message seems to be only for the very wealthy, so we could dismiss it claiming that we have no hoard of money. But as well as pleading with us on behalf of the less well off, Jesus is alerting us again to the insidious destructiveness of avarice. Those who have much want more and the more we have, the more we want. The message is clear. Wealth will never satisfy the human heart. Respectful sharing in love will always bring deeper fulfilment than the privileged acquisition that marks the lifestyle of today's successful people.

To believe that and to live accordingly is a gift of God. Today is a day to ask for it.

Nineteenth Sunday in Ordinary Time

Lk 12:32-48

Illness, or the untimely death of the talented and influential, often reminds us of how fragile is the gift of life. Yesterday's gift does not entitle us to tomorrow. Today is what we have and it cannot be hoarded. Indeed, it must be used extravagantly in the loving service of others in accordance with the intentions of the donor.

A heresy of our time is to believe that we are creatures of our own worth rather than recipients of the goodness of God. Such a heresy leads us to seek our security through our own efforts. Seeking security is a basic thrust in every human heart. When it is fulfilled, happiness is complete. When it is frustrated, despair sets in and anxiety erodes inner peace. The difference between the two is that some seek where it can never be found while others realise that it is only in God that lasting security lies.

God's fidelity is the rock on which we base our hope. God has promised to be with us always. With such a reassurance, the call is always to place our trust in God and always to be ready to answer his every call, as today's gospel challenges us to do.

Twentieth Sunday in Ordinary Time

Lk 12:49-53

Bully boys and girls run much of the world. Some are international business tycoons who can squeeze out the small operator unless he does business their way. Others are dictators who control almost the entire lives of nations whose peoples live in fear, poverty and deprivation.

Nearer home and within our homes, our workplaces, and our organisations, there is often a dominant person or group who intimidate others for their own benefit. To stand up against such intimidation, subtle or blatant, can be painful and very costly. Yet today's gospel calls on us to stand up for what we know to be right even at the risk of offending people who are close to us or who have power over us. Such a line of action requires wisdom as well as courage, sensitivity as well as strength, patience as well as perception, self-appreciation more than self-righteousness. It calls for the Spirit of God in our hearts.

Twenty-first Sunday in Ordinary Time

Lk 13:22-30

The omnipresent plastic bag is an advertising medium as well as a holdall. It does both jobs well. Children's television programmes often set out to educate as well as to entertain with a commendable degree of success. Dual purpose need not always be a barrier to effectiveness.

When listening to the gospels, it is helpful to realise that they contain both a message for the Jews of Jesus' own time and a message for every generation of believers since, including our own.

This dual focus is particularly relevant this weekend. Jesus is asked whether only a few will be saved and his reply talks of many trying to enter but only a few succeeding. This was an immediate prediction that despite all the divine preparations among the chosen people, very few of the contemporaries of Jesus would recognise him as the Messiah and fewer still would accept him as Son of God.

The perennial challenge of this gospel to each of us since is to realise that the crowd will never follow the fullness of the call of Jesus in the long run. The price of following him totally is too high for too many.

This failure has nothing to do with weakness. It is a matter of decision, of deciding to let his power act in one or not, change a person or not, awaken generosity or not, inspire courage or not, deepen faith or not. The power is God's, the decision is our own. We decide to ask God, to beg him to make us holy. The alternative is to settle for our own faltering attempts at goodness or just to follow the crowd to disappointment and disillusionment.

The choice is very stark but reassuring. God's power is never found wanting.

Twenty-second Sunday in Ordinary Time

Lk 14:1, 7-14

After the long hot summer, each one will have a memory of one's own. For many, it will be of a holiday of a lifetime with sun-drenched days by the sea. For the few, it may be of water shortage, parched crops and thirsty cattle. For others, it will be regret at having gone abroad for the sun with such glorious weather here at home. For more it will be a memory of boom business in ice cream, minerals and holiday paraphernalia. For some it will be of loss and loneliness after drownings and tragic accidents. For me, it will be of the wheel-chair holiday that I was privileged to visit.

Each year a group of volunteers in Cork undertakes the responsibility of giving a holiday away from home to more than sixty people who are confined to wheelchairs. It is the atmosphere of the holiday that strikes one. The sheer love and joy of the event almost conceal the dedication, generosity and courage of those involved. The young helpers, and indeed the not so young, blend with their guests to form a truly Christian community for the two weeks. The memory of the event came crowding back to me as I read today's gospel. 'When you give a dinner do not ask your friends or rich neighbours for fear that they repay your courtesy. When you have a party, invite the poor, the crippled, the lame, the blind; that they cannot pay you back means that you are fortunate because repayment will be made to you when the virtuous rise again.'

This gospel can be lived out. The holiday helpers were doing just that. Can we?

Twenty-third Sunday in Ordinary Time

Lk 14:25–33

We become like those we love and who love us. The truth of this adage is often observed in a loving couple who have spent so much time together during years of married life. They share the same values and are energised by doing things together. Each one's uniqueness remains but there is a real sense of unity of purpose and attitude in their approach to life. There is a common thrust in all they do. The love and care of the partner is a priority in every situation, otherwise the love would have died.

To be loved and to love is an on-going experience that changes us radically, even if sometimes imperceptibly to ourselves.

Today's gospel points out that, while following Jesus makes radical demands, it has the power to transform us. The core essential is that we put Jesus in first place, even before any legitimate affection or love. If we do so, everything will fall into place. Being loved by Jesus releases a power within us that enables us to be heroically generous and totally fulfilled in his service. The crunch factor is to allow ourselves that experience of being loved. Mistakenly, we often try to meet his somewhat frightening challenges without deepening our faith experience of his love for us.

Like the married couple, we need to spend time with him. This is what prayer is, allowing oneself to become like the one who loves you and whom you wish to love. Lovers can face any challenge together as they grow to be like each other.

Twenty-fourth Sunday in Ordinary Time

Lk 15:1-32

Anne was dreading school re-opening. Her eldest, Tony, was not yet quite five and was due to begin school on September 1. Anne feared that Tony would be afraid to leave her when they reached the school gate. She need not have worried. As soon as they came in sight of the school, he told her to go home. He would go it alone from here on in. Tony did not need his mother. She was relieved but disappointed.

It is amazing how quickly the young can discard their parents. They strike out on their own, make new friends, travel to far-away places and build new worlds. Of course, children must let go of the apron strings and make their own lives. But sometimes things do not work well. It is then that children know that parents are the ones to whom they can turn when they really need somebody. The expectation is that parents will always forgive, care, love and help. The expectations are usually fulfilled.

Christ knew this when he told the story of the prodigal son or the loving father as it is now called. Sometimes we treat God as we treat parents. We go it alone. We ignore God's plans, advice and invitations. We explore doing our own thing as a source of happiness. It does not always work out for us. Christ's message is that we always need God. God is a father to whom we can always return without fear, as our best expectations of him will be fulfilled. September is a good time for such a return.

Twenty-fifth Sunday in Ordinary Time

Lk 16:1-13

Greed, not need, is fast becoming the totally predominant consideration in deciding how the gifts of this world are distributed. This is in direct opposition to the command of Jesus that we love our neighbour as we love ourselves.

Greed is an insidious disease. It invades our hearts and lives under many disguises. Often it poses as prudence in providing for future emergencies that may never happen. More subtly, it justifies itself on the plea that we need a little more comfort and security as middle age steals over us. More dangerously still, it suggests that as everybody else is looking after their own selfish interests, it must be right and good to do so. Almost unnoticed, money and what it can buy becomes our god and we become idolaters.

In today's gospel, Jesus highlights the urgency of choosing which god we wish to follow, money or the true God. One cannot choose both. Earlier, Amos condemns the sharp practices that greed nourishes when it is allowed to take root in our daily lifestyle. Like weeds or scutch grass, its eradication is never easy.

Twenty-sixth Sunday in Ordinary Time

Lk 16:19-31

Concern for one's own people is a very strong characteristic among us. So, Dives, the hapless rich man in today's gospel story, could well hail from this part of the country. Even when all was lost for himself, he was anxious to see his brothers fixed up better than he had been. He had failed to take even his obvious opportunities to help the needy and his indifference had deprived him of the possibility of sharing heaven with his less fortunate neighbours. To protect the brothers from a similar fate, he pleaded with Abraham to send a messenger from the dead to warn them. The reply was stark. If people choose not to listen to God's message and his messengers, they will not heed even one who rises from the dead.

Jesus was foretelling his own resurrection and pointing out that despite even this climax to his miracles, many would refuse to believe or to live according to his message. It is a common danger that we only hear what suits us and that we block out anything that questions our comfort or our complacency.

In all our lives there are Dives situations where we choose to ignore even the most obvious of gospel challenges. Today is an invitation to look again at the Lazarus on our doorstep.

Twenty-seventh Sunday in Ordinary Time

Lk 17:5-10

For the birdwatcher, binoculars are essential. For the botanist, the magnifying glass is the constant companion. For both, their enjoyment of the wonder of the world is enhanced beyond measure by means of their chosen lens. This carefully-prepared lens reveals aspects of reality kept hidden from the casual observer. It allows the user to explore creation from another perspective, almost as an insider. Such a lens needs to be protected, cleaned and adjusted to remain fully effective.

Faith can be likened to a lens that God gives believers to explore that fullness of his plan for us. It enables us to experience the richness of God's embracing love from within as one of the family. To live without the lens of faith is to live on the surface of reality unaware of the wonder of God. To see things with a faith perspective is a gift of God to be pleaded for, protected, nourished and treasured.

Yet faith is much more than a life lens. As well as enhancing the view, faith actually changes the viewer. Faith is the foundation stone on which love is built. Faith-filled love transforms the relationship between the creator and the created one. It is the source of all our hope. It cannot be hoarded since it is through sharing it with others that it is deepened in our own hearts. So every believer must sow seeds of goodness in every nook and cranny of daily life. Such is our glorious calling. As Jesus puts it in today's gospel, no matter how small the seed, it will bear fruit beyond measure if it is sown in faith. To settle for less is to betray our inheritance.

Twenty-eighth Sunday in Ordinary Time

Lk 17:11-19

Gospel stories often have two messages, one obvious and the other less so. Today's gospel is no exception. Having cured the ten lepers, Jesus is very hurt that nine out of the ten did not bother to say thanks. Our immediate reaction is to protest that we would not be so blatantly ungrateful. Of course, the truth is that just as the nine took it for granted that a healer's job is to heal, we often take God's gifts and many others' goodness to us for granted and sail through the day unaware of our lack of appreciation. Such is our self-centredness.

But there is a more profound message in this gospel as well. It tells how the healing happened. The lepers did what Jesus asked of them. Sometimes we look for healing from sin, selfishness, unforgivingness, anxious fear or some other trouble, but we refuse to do what Jesus asks of us. Today's gospel is an invitation to put our needs before Jesus, but we must listen honestly to what he is clearly asking of us and, like the Samaritan, act accordingly.

Twenty-ninth Sunday in Ordinary Time

Lk 18:1-8

One of the encouraging blessings of priestly parish life is frequent contact with people who trust in the Lord and never lose heart despite the most trying circumstances of deprivation, ill-health, broken relationships, family troubles or bereavement. Today's gospel challenges us to be like such people and to sustain ourselves in the struggle through persevering prayer. A role model for such perseverance is Mary at the foot of the cross. She stands there as her one and only innocent son is being executed as a criminal in the most horrendous circumstances. She did not know that there was going to be a resurrection, but she trusted God to be with her as he had called her. Her strength was the love she shared with her son, his love for her and her love for him. It was a love that was born and nurtured in daily contact with Jesus and in shared family prayer to the Father. In this way she had become secure in the love of God for her and this love sustained her through the pain.

It is only this same love that can sustain us in difficult times. We need to believe that God loves each of us individually with an unfailing love. Such vibrant faith is a gift of God for which we must ask unflinchingly, day in, day out, knowing that God never ignores such pleas. We need never lose heart.

Thirtieth Sunday in Ordinary Time

Lk 18:9-14

Pretence starts early in life with the pressure to keep up appearances. Children are sometimes taught to let on that things are better at home than they really are. Appearances count for more than truth does. Honesty, especially about one's feelings, may be alright but must be kept in its place, a very private place. Pretence can so easily become a way of life. Most people engage in a little sometimes.

Children are experts at it, but they usually know when they are pretending and hopefully grow out of it as they mature. Pretending adults can grow into their pretences with tragic consequences.

This is what happened to the Pharisee in today's gospel. He was so long putting up a front of honesty, self-righteousness and religious practice that he began to believe that he was humankind's gift to God. He lost all awareness of his need of God. There is no greater loss.

On the other hand, the tax collector recognised his failings honestly within himself and so was open to receive the enabling merciful love of God. In this way he was restored, redeemed and saved. Inner personal honesty was the crucial inner peace. Things have not changed.

Thirty-first Sunday in Ordinary Time

Lk 19:1-10

Curiosity is a two-edged sword. As every schoolboy knows, idle curiosity can lead one into all sorts of trouble. On the other hand, it was curiosity that led Columbus to find America and led Fleming to discover penicillin. Indeed, curiosity has not only led to the great discoveries of human history but it has unexpectedly and completely changed the lives of some persons who impulsively followed a whim of curiosity.

Zacchaeus was one such person. He was simply curious about Jesus and wondered what the great preacher looked like. To sneak a glance at him as he passed by, Zacchaeus climbed a sycamore tree, not thinking for a moment that Jesus would have any interest in him. After all, Jesus was a committed Jew, faithful to the law, to his people and their customs.

As against that, Zacchaeus had collaborated with the foreign forces of occupation and done very well out of it financially. His own Jewish people had ostracised him for that betrayal and he thought that Jesus would be no different.

But Jesus was different. He saw Zacchaeus. Their eyes met and, in the meeting, Jesus invited Zacchaeus to meet his God again and to make a new beginning. Zacchaeus took the ball on the hop. It was a chance that might not come again. He started immediately to put things right and to make amends.

Today can be our opportunity to meet Jesus. We all need to make the most of the Zacchaeus moments in our lives.

Thirty-second Sunday in Ordinary Time

Lk 20:27-38

There are two ways of putting a question. One way is to ask in the hope of getting a genuinely helpful answer. The purpose of the other way is to put the person questioned on a spot, to trap him or her in ignorance or foolishness or both. It was in this latter frame of mind that the Sadducees approached Jesus with a question about the resurrection.

They had their minds made up and were determined to score a point, downing anybody with a different viewpoint. As a result, they could not open their minds and hearts to listen to the one who was to be the first to experience resurrection, the core of their questioning.

They were asking the right person but their certainty about their position prevented them hearing God's newly-revealed message, which was to transform their traditional but static view of the after-life.

Jesus came not with a blueprint of precise detail about the next life but with a vision of how we could now begin to live a life of love with God and with each other, which will blossom after death in ways totally beyond our present understanding. Jesus came to enable us to live such a life.

Today's gospel is a reminder that the teaching of Jesus is a call to trust in the caring wisdom of the Father, to believe that all creation is safely in his hands, to realise that he is always leading us to find him in new ways in a rapidly-changing world, to know that every person is alive with God always.

The temptation is to reduce this core of faith to the limitation of what we can understand. The fate of the Sadducees was to succumb to this temptation. It can happen to any of us.

Thirty-third Sunday in Ordinary Time

Lk 21:5-19

In time of hardship or serious illness, the usual prayer and hope is that the difficulty be taken away. The more common aspiration is for a cure. There is an alternative hope and approach. It is to ask for the strength and support, for the fortitude to live out the trial or pain while having inner peace in one's heart. To be able to do so is a gift of God.

Today's gospel is a reminder that God does give such a gift. The suggestion is that we ask for it. Such asking can only be done by people of faith. The merely human approach is to see the removal of pain as the only solution. But the follower of Jesus knows that when we entrust ourselves to God, the cross can be fruitfully borne and indeed must be borne to be with God.

A malaise of our time is to seek instant ease even if it destroys our road to true fulfilment. The gospel message is that the gift of endurance will bring us eternal life. It is a gift worth seeking.

Our Lord Jesus Christ, Universal King

(Thirty-fourth Sunday in Ordinary Time)

Lk 23:35-43

'Jesus, remember me when you come into your kingdom.' This prayer of the good thief is fascinating not only in its effectiveness but in its origins. Judging by appearances, the three being crucified were all going to suffer the same fate. Certainly, the other thief had no doubt that it was all over for the three of them and gave vent to his frustrated desperate anger accordingly. What stirred the other criminal dying on a cross to believe that the man on the next cross could have any power to help?

Somehow, in some faltering way, there was a spark of faith, a fleeting glimpse that Jesus was more than he seemed, that he could and would help. So arose the heartfelt plea, 'remember me'. It is a plea re-echoed in many hearts over the years since.

To be remembered is the cornerstone of relationships. It is how friendship is nurtured and blossoms. Remembrance makes present again the reality of the bond between separated or absent friends. Without it, there is no hope. To experience being remembered is a blessing to be treasured and drawn upon in the darker moments. Just as this is true of human love and friendship, it is particularly true of our relationship with Jesus. Indeed, as the good thief's prayer brought an instant guaranteed promise of everlasting friendship, today's gospel assures us of a similar outcome when we make this prayer our own. It can be in our hearts and on our lips every day all day. It has the potential to link us with Jesus unceasingly.

'Jesus, remember me' is an aspiration for the sinner rather than for the saint. We can feel at home with it.

St Patrick's Day

Lk 10:1-12, 17-20

Shamrock and St Patrick's Day are inextricably linked in our tradition. Long before we adopted our national flag, the shamrock evoked strong feelings in many hearts about Ireland and matters Irish. Some feelings are nostalgic for the emigrant's homeland. Some are patriotic, articulating a yearning for freedom. Some are cultural, linking with our rich Gaelic heritage. Some are religious, reminding us of the faith that Patrick brought.

The origin of our shamrock tradition is found in the story that Patrick picked a shamrock to illustrate the core of our faith that in our God, Father, Son and Holy Spirit are three persons in one God. It is a faith that has formed us over generations into a people. It is a faith that our people have not only taken with them all over the world but which has taken our missionaries to the ends of the earth. It is a faith that is celebrated and renewed every Holy Week and Easter when we remember that the Son, sent by the Father and imbued by the Holy Spirit, suffered, died and rose from the dead, so that we would share fully in the life of God himself. Palm Sunday begins our great remembrance when Jesus arrives triumphantly into Jerusalem, the scene of his execution and his glory.

To wear the shamrock, is to acknowledge that we are Irish and inheritors of a valued tapestry of faith, of generous care for each other, and of respect for the weak and oppressed. To hold the palm aloft is to pledge allegiance to the Christ whom Patrick made known to those who went before us.

The Assumption of the Blessed Virgin Mary

Lk 1:39-56

Young babies have an unending fascination for many people. Some try to spot the inherited looks. Others look for premature signs of greatness, often to the embarrassment of parents who just want to treasure their child now without outside speculation about the future. Such speculation was forced on Mary and Joseph from the beginning as the shepherds recounted the signs that accompanied the birth of Jesus.

For the parents, it had been a normal enough birth with all the discomforts and inconveniences that are the usual lot of the very poor. But the shepherds insisted that angels had told them that Jesus was to be saviour of the world. The frugality of the stable gave little indication of such future greatness.

Yet, like many parents, Mary and Joseph believed in the God-given destiny of their child whatever it was to be.

To believe in the precious destiny of each child is at the core of fulfilling parenting, both its joy and its challenge. To lose faith in one's offspring is to amputate part of oneself and to cripple the development of those entrusted to us. It can happen through substituting our own ambitions for the unique niche which God has created for each child.

Like all Jewish mothers, Mary must have had her own hopes for her Messiah son. But to her eternal credit, she trusted the Father to reveal in time the role for which Jesus was destined.

Her trust was tested especially at Calvary and rewarded uniquely at her assumption.

Mission Sunday

Lk 5:1-12

For many Irish people a great deal of world news has a very personal dimension. The initial shock of the Gulf crisis was heightened by bonds of friendship or acquaintance with the stranded ones. The armed conflict in famine-stricken Ethiopia endangers our heroic relief workers and nuns. The barbarity of the civil strife in Liberia destroyed many mission stations of our priests and sisters, evoking a heroism among them above and beyond the call of duty. In the Philippines, vested wealthy interests strive constantly to eliminate those who work to build up God's kingdom as the Niall O'Brien saga showed us. Indeed, it seems that it is especially when the people involved are under attack or that their work is being destroyed that we appreciate the thousands of Irish women and men, lay and religious, who are scattered worldwide as missionaries of the gospel of Jesus Christ.

Mission Sunday is a focus day for the home churches to link with our missionary brothers and sisters. Some people will write the letter of interest and encouragement to these apostles abroad who have followed the more radical call. Most will pray God's blessing on them and their work which fulfils for all of us Christ's command to bring salvation to all the world. Hopefully, many will dig deep into their pockets and purses, sacrificing their own enjoyment for a week or more to give missionaries what they need for their God-given task.

Mission Sunday can touch each of us so that our faith is strengthened, missionary vocations are awakened and fostered, while those who have left homeland to follow Christ will be encouraged in their calling. Our generosity on the day is one measure of our gratitude for God's love. It will tell its own story.

All Saints

Mt 5:1-12

The young boys play football on the side of the city street. It is their only pitch. Their nimble feet cope with weaving walkers and murmuring motorists. Other youngsters may have safe and finer pitches but they all share the same vision. They dream of playing with Manchester or Ipswich. (It used to be Liverpool.) But while nourishing that dream, they play their hearts out in today's game, viewing the here and now as all important.

It is much the same for Christians. We have a dream; a vision of being with God forever in heaven. But Christianity demands that we live the present as all-important and believing that those who strive for what is right will be satisfied.

Today, the Feast of All Saints, we remember those who have reached the fulfilment of the dream. Today, our task is to live fully alive, inspired by the trust that the merciful will obtain and that peacemakers will be called children of God.

The Immaculate Conception

Lk 1:26-38

A children's concert always fascinates me. I mean a concert where the children perform. I find myself marvelling at the uniqueness of each child. The songs may be hackneyed or just composed. In each case, the child performer brings something very personal to the item. It may be joy, anxiety, enthusiasm, genius or just ordinary happiness. The kernel is that it is the child's unique contribution that makes it all worthwhile and the concert is not the same for any two children.

The Father chose to entrust his Son to a young girl, Mary. An amazing choice, surely. Once chosen he prepared her for the role and life as Mother of Christ. Mary's response was confident and concerned. Despite the difficulties of Joseph's doubts and neighbours' gossip, she trusted the God who had chosen her to be with her each step of the way. Her practical concern showed itself immediately as she moved to help Elizabeth.

The same God entrusts the same Jesus Christ to each of us. This individual choice becomes more amazing. Really, if the Almighty God wants to fulfil his plans by sending his Son among us, that is his privilege. The extraordinary thing is that he did it especially for me. I never cease to wonder that the coming of the Son of God and the unique preparation of Mary for that event are part of God's plan of love for me. To each person God gives a unique personal gift and invitation. The choice is God's. The response is ours. Each person's unique contribution makes God present in our world.